I0201170

MISSIONS AND MISSIONARIES OF THE FREE METHODIST CHURCH

By

B. WINGET

First Fruits Press
Wilmore, Kentucky
c2016

Missions and Missionaries of the Free Methodist Church. By B. Winget.

First Fruits Press, ©2016
Previously published by the Free Methodist Publishing House, ©1911
ISBN: 9781621714804 (print) 9781621714811 (digital) 9781621714828 (kindle)
Digital version at http://place.asburyseminary.edu/freemethodistbooks/9/

First Fruits Press is a digital imprint of the Asbury Theological Seminary, B.L. Fisher Library. Asbury Theological Seminary is the legal owner of the material previously published by the Pentecostal Publishing Co. and reserves the right to release new editions of this material as well as new material produced by Asbury Theological Seminary. Its publications are available for noncommercial and educational uses, such as research, teaching and private study. First Fruits Press has licensed the digital version of this work under the Creative Commons Attribution Noncommercial 3.0 United States License. To view a copy of this license, visit http://creativecommons.org/licenses/by-nc/3.0/us/.

For all other uses, contact:

First Fruits Press
B.L. Fisher Library
Asbury Theological Seminary
204 N. Lexington Ave.
Wilmore, KY 40390
http://place.asburyseminary.edu/firstfruits

Winget, B.

    Missions and Missionaries of the Free Methodist Church / by B. Winget. --
    Wilmore, Kentucky : First Fruits Press, ©2016.
    124 pages: illustrations, portraits; 21 cm.
    Reprint. Previously published: Chicago: Free Methodist Publishing House,
    © 1911. Includes index.
    ISBN: 9781621714804 (pbk.)

    1. Free Methodist Church of North America -- Missions--History.
      2. Missionaries--Biography. I. Title.

BV2550. W56 2016   266.79

Cover design by Jonathan Ramsay

asburyseminary.edu
800.2ASBURY
204 North Lexington Avenue
Wilmore, Kentucky 40390

First Fruits
THE ACADEMIC OPEN PRESS OF ASBURY SEMINARY

First Fruits Press
The Academic Open Press of Asbury Theological Seminary
204 N. Lexington Ave., Wilmore, KY 40390
859-858-2236
first.fruits@asburyseminary.edu
asbury.to/firstfruits

Yours truly
B. Winget

MISSIONS *and* MISSIONARIES

of the Free Methodist Church

By Rev. B. Winget

Chicago
FREE METHODIST PUBLISHING HOUSE
1911

TO OUR
MISSIONARIES

INTRODUCTION

The Free Methodist church had its origin in a special out-pouring of the Spirit, so it is natural that she should be endued with great missionary zeal. This spirit of missions was shown in the beginning of her history by going into the highways and hedges—holding religious services in schoolhouses, private homes, barns, on the streets, in dance halls and in groves—and compelling the people to come to the gospel feast.

Beginning thus at Jerusalem (when the church was organized) it was but natural that the spirit of holiness and missions should lead the church to bear witness in Samaria —distant parts of our own land, and on to the uttermost parts of the earth.

How small were the beginnings of our missionary work— two missionaries, no Board, no funds provided by the church. Then comes a Missionary Board, incorporated, appeals for funds, and our first missionaries sent out to Africa.

From a few dollars raised we now raise our tens of thousands. We have our Woman's Foreign Missionary Societies, our Junior Societies, and men, women and children everywhere helping by prayer and means to carry the gospel to those who sit in heathen night.

We trust that the pages of this little book may be interesting, helpful and instructive. May we all feel our hearts and lips touched with hallowed fire from off the altar of Jehovah. Let us look on the fields, pray for the laborers to be sent out, give of our means for their going, and say from our hearts, "Here am I, send me."

ORGANIZATION

The General Conference, held at Burlington, Iowa, October 11-22, 1882, made disciplinary provision for a General Conference Missionary Board. At that time the following were elected members of this Board: Rev. J. Travis, editor

REV. CHARLES B. EBEY
Born, May 16, 1847   Died, June 17, 1908
Missionary Secretary, 1882-1890

of the *Free Methodist;* Rev. D. M. Sinclair, of the Wisconsin conference; Rev. W. W. Kelley, of the Central Illinois conference; Revs. J. G. Terrill, C. B. Ebey and T. B. Arnold, of the Illinois conference, and D. W. Abrams, of the Michigan conference.

On Monday, October 22, 1882, these brethren met and organized by electing J. Travis, president; T. B. Arnold, treasurer. C. B. Ebey had already been elected general secretary by the General Conference.

The Missionary Board was incorporated, June 19, 1885,

under the name of General Missionary Board of the Free Methodist church.

On March 15, 1895, the corporate name was changed to read, "General Missionary Board of the Free Methodist

REV. WALTER W. KELLEY
Born, May 11, 1841   Died, May 17, 1899
Missionary Secretary, 1890-1893

Church of North America." At the same time two paragraphs were added to the certificate of incorporation, giving the Board enlarged powers, and the management of the busi ness was vested in a Board of five directors instead of five trustees as formerly. April 18, 1908, a further change was made by providing for seven instead of five directors.

Woman's Foreign Missionary Society

The first local Woman's Foreign Missionary Society was organized in 1882; the second one in 1890.

The General Woman's Foreign Missionary Society was organized in 1894. Previous to this time, 1890-1894, conference, district and local societies had been organized. Mrs. Ellen Lois Roberts was elected first president of the General Society, and Mrs. Mary L. Coleman the second and present occupant of that office.

Secretaries of the Board

Rev Charles Bond Ebey has the honor of being the first Missionary Secretary. He was elected by the General Confer

REV. JOSEPH G. TERRILL
Born, September 6, 1838   Died, April 23, 1895
Missionary Secretary, 1893-1895

ence held at Burlington, Iowa, October 11-22, 1882. He held the office until the fall of 1890. Rev. W. W. Kelley, assistant secretary, having resigned in November, 1889, Rev. Thomas B. Arnold was elected to fill out his term.

Rev. Walter W. Kelley was elected Missionary Secretary in the fall of 1890. In April, 1893, he resigned and Rev. Joseph G. Terrill was appointed to fill the place.

Brother Terrill died in the spring of 1895, and in July

following Rev. Benjamin Winget was elected to the office by
the executive committee.

In the spring of 1898, because of a crisis in the missionary
work in Africa, the Board requested Brother Winget to visit
that field. He sailed from New York April first. In the latter part of 1900, for similar reasons, he was sent to India,
and from there to Japan, thus making a tour around the
world.

In July, 1907, accompanied by Mrs. Winget, he visited
the mission field in the Dominican Republic. While there he
had charge of the first Christian Convention ever held in the
interior of the island.

Brother Winget has been reelected by three successive
general conferences, and is the present incumbent of the office.

FUNDS RAISED

From Individuals and Societies

The first record we have of money raised for foreign missions was in 1883, and the amount was $42.35. The amount reported the next year—1884—was $504.48.

The amount raised by quadrenniums from 1883 to 1895 was as follows:

For quadrennium closing 1886	$ 3,805.96
For quadrennium closing 1890	4,971.04
For quadrennium closing 1894	12,919.18
For quadrennium closing 1898	17,065.93
For quadrennium closing 1902	16,510.92
For quadrennium closing 1906	31,731.79
For quadrennium closing 1910	45,196.62
Total	$132,201.44

Through Woman's Foreign Missionary Society

Funds sent quadrennially into the general treasury of the Woman's Foreign Missionary Society from October 1, 1894, to October 1, 1910, are as follows:

For quadrennium closing 1898	$ 18,920.47
For quadrennium closing 1902	45,673.19
For quadrennium closing 1906	96,297.11
For quadrennium closing 1910	166,401.64
Total	$327,292.41
Grand total	$459,493.85

AFRICA

G. Harry and Mrs. Lillie Smith Agnew

G. Harry Agnew was accepted by the Board and went out to Africa in the spring of 1885, arriving at Inhambane on the southeast coast, June 17. He remained in Africa four years, returning home in January, 1889. He embarked again for Africa in July, 1890. His associates in the work, Rev. W. W. Kelley and wife, came home after being in Africa about a year, and he was left alone on that field until the arrival of the missionaries who went out March 3, 1888. During that time he suffered severe tests and hardships, having poor accommodations for living, and no associates of our own Board as companions and helpers. He returned to America the second time in September, 1894, attending the General Conference which was held in October of that year. He remained in this country only a few months and again returned to Africa. Three weeks after his arrival there he married Susie Sherman, February 3, 1895, at the Fair View Mission Station, and a little later they went to Inhambane. Their married life was brief, as Sister Agnew died of fever on the 17th of the following December.

The unhealthfulness of the climate at Inhambane necessitated a change, and in 1897 Brother Agnew went to Johannesburg to live, having labored at Inhambane for about twelve years. On May 3, 1897, he was married to Lillie Smith. As the fruit of his work at Johannesburg we have two mission houses, and his labors there have been rewarded with encouraging spiritual results. During the Boer-English War, for about two and one-half years, it became necessary for him to suspend his labors at Johannesburg. During that time he assisted in the work at Natal, especially in opening the new station at what was then called Ebenezer. At the close of the war he returned to Johannesburg and was in charge of the work there and also at Inhambane. Brother Agnew died at Germiston, South Africa, March 9, 1903, leaving a wife and two children, Susie and G. Harry.

Soon after the death of Brother Agnew, his wife, accompanied by her children and a native named Peter Magubeni, came to America, arriving in New York, May 23, 1903. Peter attended our seminary at Spring Arbor, Michigan, while they were in America, and traveled with Sister Agnew and others, assisting in missionary services, speaking through an interpreter. He made a very favorable impression upon our people because of his humility and piety, as well as by his native ability. The labors of Sister Agnew and Peter in the interests of missionary work in Africa were especially blessed of the Lord and fruitful in results while they remained in America. They embarked at New York for Africa, May 27, 1907.

Peter's work was short after he reached Africa, as he was taken away by death before he realized his hopes in regard to giving the gospel message to his people, the Machopis. He has, however, left a legacy of faithfulness and devotion to the Master's service for the work in Africa, as well as the church in America. Since Mrs. Agnew's return she has labored the most of the time at, or near, Fair View, Natal, South Africa. For a time she acted as pastor of the work at Fair View Mission Station and there was a gracious outpouring of the Spirit during her pastorate, and much fruit was gathered in. She is now in charge of an out-station at Magog, a few miles from Fair View, and is laboring zealously and faithfully for the Master, with some encouragement and fruit.

Rev. W. W. and Mrs. Augusta Tullis Kelley

Rev. W. W. Kelley and wife, of the Central Illinois conference, were accepted by the Board and sent out to Africa, leaving New York City, April 25, 1885, and arriving at Inhambane, June 17, 1885. On account of his failing health they returned to America in about a year.

Mr. and Mrs. Robert R. Shemeld

Robert R. Shemeld and wife were accepted by the Board and went out to Africa with Rev. and Mrs. W. W. Kelley and G. H. Agnew. They arrived at Durban, Natal, in the early part of June, 1885, going inland to Estcourt, where they started a mission, afterward known as Bethany Mission. They returned home in the early part of 1890, and he attended a

Board meeting held April 24th of that year. At this meeting he offered his resignation to the Board. A committee appointed by the Board requested him to recall his resignation, receive his credentials, and return to Estcourt. Not complying with this request, when the board adjourned his case was left with the Executive Committee. Later he proposed to purchase the Bethany Mission property and the Board voted to lease it to him for a nominal sum. He returned to Africa and was at Bethany for a time. At a meeting of the Board held October 17, 1893, the following action was taken: "On motion, the office of Robert Shemeld as trustee of the Mission property at Bethany, Zulu Mission, is declared vacant, he having ceased to work under the Board and having vacated the property." His relation to the Board was discontinued.

Miss Mary E. Carpenter

Mary E. Carpenter, of New York State, went out to Liberia, West Africa, as a Board missionary, leaving New York City, September 12, 1885. She reached Liberia on Thanksgiving Day. Her services for the Master on that trying field were short, as she died January 3, 1886. She was a woman of estimable character and greatly beloved.

Rev. and Mrs. A. D. Noyes

Rev. and Mrs. A. D. Noyes went out to Liberia, West Africa, under the Board, leaving New York, September 12, 1885. They returned to America, May 23, 1896. Brother and Sister Noyes were again sent out under the Board to labor in Natal, arriving at Durban, November 29, 1887. They worked only ten weeks under the Board and during that time were with Brother Shemeld at the Bethany Mission Station. As the Board failed to send the needed means for their support, they labored for three years under the American Board. They resumed work under our Board, December 1, 1890, and continued in its employ until the fall of 1898. He was home on a short visit in the fall of 1895, arriving in New York City, October 7 to attend the annual Board meeting. At this meeting an agreement was reached between him and the Board for the transfer of the Fair View Mission property to the Board, and on the 9th of November following he left New York for Natal. They remained there until August 31, 1898, when they returned to America and ceased to labor under the Board. While in Africa their labors were successful in securing the very desirable property at Fair View, which was turned over to the Missionary Board and is now the headquarters of our work in Africa.

Miss F. Grace Allen

Miss Allen sailed for Africa, March 3, 1888, in company with five other missionaries, and reached that field April 30. Her first work in Africa was at Inhambane, where she labored three months with our missionaries. She then taught a Boys' and Girls' School for the American Board for one year, being at Inhambane in all fifteen months. She went to Natal in August, 1889, and as our Board had no mission there where she could stay, and had not made sufficient provision for her, she took work under the American Board at Inanda, remaining there as a teacher in the Native Girls' Seminary for two years. In August, 1891, she went to Fair View Mission Station which has since been her field of labor. Her principal work has been teaching. She had charge of the station school at first, but later organized and took charge of a Girls' School and Home. In September, 1894, she left for America, and returned June 10, 1895. In August, 1906, she again returned to the home land, where she remained until November 2, 1907, when she returned with a small company of new missionaries.

Miss Allen was in charge of the station school at Fair View, Natal, for several years after reaching that place, but about the year 1897 she organized the Girls' School at Fair View. Speaking of this school she says, "God has set His seal of blessing and approval upon it since its first commencement with two or three heathen girls." At the present time there are 144 girls enrolled in the school. Of all our missionaries in Africa Miss Allen has been longest on the field, and her self-denying labors and faithful services are highly appreciated both there and in the home land.

Rev. and Mrs. J. D. Bennett

Rev. J. D. Bennett and wife, of the East Michigan conference, having been accepted by the Board, embarked from New York for Africa, March 3, 1888, arriving there April 30. They labored about two years under our Board and about one year and eight months under the American Board. They returned to America, November 1, 1893. At a meeting of the sub-committee of the Missionary Board, March 25, 1889, J. D. Bennett's resignation, which had previously been tendered to the Board, was considered and accepted. They were reappointed by the Board, April 5, 1893, to go to Inhambane in 1894. At the annual meeting of the Board, held October 17, 1893, this action was rescinded.

Mrs. Ida Heffner Spalding

Miss Heffner was accepted by the Board and embarked at New York for Africa, March 3, 1888. She reached there April 30, and labored about seven months under our Board, and nearly four and a half years under the American Board. She returned to America in March, 1893, and her relation to the Board was discontinued. She was married to Mr. Frank Spalding, June 7, 1900.

A. D. and Mrs. Abbie Lincoln

Mr. A. D. Lincoln and wife were accepted by the Board and left New York for Africa, March 3, 1888, arriving there April 30. They went to Komeni Mission Station, about fifty miles from Inhambane, where she passed to her heavenly reward June 20, 1888. After her death he started with his little girl, Edith, for America. He was suffering with fever at the time, and stopped at Bethany Mission with Brother Shemeld, where he died July 29, 1888. Edith was brought to America later.

C. N. Taylor

C. N. Taylor was accepted by the Board, November 4, 1891. Later the Board voted that he be ordained in view of his going out to the foreign field. At the time J. D. Bennett and wife were reaccepted for Inhambane, C. N. Taylor's going out was deferred until 1894. At the annual meeting of the Board, October 17, 1893, the Board rescinded its action in regard to sending out Brother Taylor. The reasons for this action were that J. D. Bennett and wife did not go, and it was thought that Brother Taylor's health was not sufficient for the work of a foreign missionary.

Rev. and Mrs. J. J. Haviland

Rev. J. J. Haviland, Frank L. Desh, Emma Hillmon and Rose Myers were accepted by the Board and embarked at New York for South Africa, arriving there in May, 1892. J. J. Haviland and Emma Hillmon were married at Estcourt, Natal, October 28. 1892. After their marriage they remained at Bethany Mission, Estcourt, until the property was sold, and went from there to Inhambane, June 13, 1895. They remained there until his death, which occurred March 18, 1897, just as they were about to return to America. A few days after his death, Mrs. Haviland with her two children took ship for America, arriving in May. They labored diligently and faithfully while in Africa, and his sudden and unexpected death was deeply felt. After her arrival in America, as health and family cares would permit, she traveled and spoke on missions in the interest of our foreign work. Her relation to the Board was continued until October, 1900.

Frank L. and Rose Myers Desh

Frank L. Desh and Rose Myers were married in the chapel at Fair View, July 4, 1892. They left there for Inhambane, November 7, 1892. Their stay in that place was short, and they returned to Natal. They engaged in rescue mission work in Durban, Natal, contrary to the direction of the Board, which resulted in the discontinuance of their relations to the Board. They returned to America in 1898.

Anna L. Witteman and Laura J. Morse

Anna L. Witteman, of Kansas, and Laura J. Morse, of Iowa, were accepted for Africa at a meeting of the Directors

of the Missionary Board, held January 7, 1897. Miss Witte
man's health failed the following August so that she was unable to go, and, although Laura J. Morse had furnished what
was considered a proper health certificate when she was accepted by the Directors, the Secretary learned later that her
father could not secure such a health certificate as would enable him to get her life insured. For this and other reasons the
Board, at its annual meeting held in October, rescinded its
former action in appointing her to go out to Africa.

John Pearson and Anna C. Sanford Brodhead

John Pearson Brodhead and wife left New York for Fair
View, Natal, South Africa, April 6, 1898, and arrived at Durban, Natal, May 15. Before going out both Mr. and Mrs.
Brodhead spent a few months studying the Zulu language un
der the instruction of Mrs. Emma Hillmon Haviland.

Brother Brodhead was converted in his eighteenth year, and
soon after united with the Methodist Episcopal church at
Franklin, Pennsylvania. He was licensed by that body as a
local preacher, January 3, 1890. He married Miss Anna C.
Sanford in October, 1891. In May, 1892, he united with the
Free Methodist church and was granted an exhorter's license.
At the ensuing session of the quarterly conference he was
granted a local preacher's license and recommended to the
traveling connection. Later he went from Pennsylvania to
Greenville College, Illinois, where Mrs. Brodhead had been
employed as art teacher. In the fall of 1892 he joined the Central Illinois conference on trial and took work for one year.
The following year he was left without work in order to finish
his studies at Greenville College, but during the last half of
the year he supplied work at Fallston and Beaver Falls, Pennsylvania. At the session of the Central Illinois conference of
1894 he was granted a transfer to the Pittsburg conference,
where he labored until accepted as a missionary to Africa. He was ordained deacon in 1894 and elder in 1897. At
the session of conference in 1900 he was granted a transfer to
the Oil City conference. Upon arriving in Africa, Brother
Brodhead was given charge of the work at Natal and was
superintendent of the work there until the organization
of the South Africa Mission conference, by Bishop Sel-

lew at Fair View, Natal, South Africa, October 11-16, 1905.
For the first two years after the organization of the conference Brother Brodhead filled the office of district elder over
the whole conference. With zeal and diligence he endeavored
to enlarge the work. In so doing he was subject to depriva-
tions and tests, which affected his health, and because of this
he and Mrs. Brodhead were granted a furlough.

At the time of their going out Brother and Sister Brodhead had two little daughters, whom they left with Sister
Brodhead's mother and sister in America for two years. At
the end of that time the mother, who was seventy-seven
years of age, and the sister, Miss Hattie Sanford, went out to
Africa with the children, and remained on the field until
Brother and Sister Brodhead returned in the spring of 1907,
when they also returned. They left Durban, April 11. On
the 24th they crossed the equator, and the day following
Mother Sanford had her eighty-fourth birthday. During the
seven years she spent in Africa she enjoyed good health and
did excellent service for the Master. She is still well
preserved. A native girl by the name of Elizabeth Nom-
bango Zelemu also accompanied them home and remained
in this country for a year or more, attending school,
and then returned to Africa, where she is now engaged as
teacher in the Girls' School at Fair View. Brother Brodhead
and family returned to Africa in December, 1909. He opened
a new station in Pondoland, and assisted in opening several
others in Natal and one in East Griqualand. Since his return he has also opened our work in the Critchlow Mission
Station, in Pondoland, and has charge of it, and is also acting
as district elder of the Coast district of the South Africa conference.

Miss Lucy A. Hartman

Miss Hartman left New York for Africa, April 6, 1898,
and arrived at Durban, Natal, South Africa, May 15. She
was converted at the age of ten years and spent three years
in Wessington Springs Seminary preparing for missionary
work. After eleven years of hard work on the foreign
field, she returned to the home land in the spring of 1909.

She remained until August 31, 1910, when she again embarked
for Africa, accompanied by Miss Maud Cretors, of the Men-
nonite church, who had previously labored with her for some
years. Some of Miss Hartman's time in Africa has been spent
in teaching, but the most of it in evangelistic labors at Ebenezer and Itemba Mission Stations. Her labors have been
fruitful in results, and an encouraging number, among whom
are some heathen who are well along in years, have found the
light of life through her prayers and labors.

W. C. and Mrs. Viola Gray

W. C. Gray and wife were accepted by the Board, October
12, 1899, and appointed to go out to Africa, not later than
April 1, 1900. Mrs. Sanford and her daughter, Miss Hattie,
with the two children of Mr. and Mrs. J. P. Brodhead, accompanied them to Africa. He was given the industrial work
in connection with our land at Fair View, Natal, South Africa.

They embarked at New York for their field of labor in the
spring of 1900. They labored zealously in the work given
them for a short time, but because of unfaithfulness on his
part, he was discontinued by the action of the Directors and
Secretary, June 16, 1903. At the same time that he was discontinued, Sister Gray sent in her resignation which was accepted by the Secretary. They remained in Africa for several years, but later returned to America.

Miss Margaret A. Nickel

Miss Nickel, having been accepted by the Board for Africa,
on April 4, 1902, in company with Miss Rosa Hunter, Nathanael B. Smith and wife and Carroll Smith, embarked from
New York for South Africa. She joined the Free Methodist
church when but nine years of age. Being persuaded that God
had called her to the foreign field, she entered the Southern
California University of the Methodist Episcopal church in
the fall of 1896 and continued in that school for one year.
In 1898 she entered Wessington Springs Seminary, where she
studied more than a year, but left because of the illness of her

mother. For eight years Miss Nickel has toiled in evangelistic work, principally on new stations, and has been rewarded by seeing precious souls saved. The most of the time she has been associated with Miss Hartman in the work. Failing health made it necessary for her to come home in the summer of 1910. Since her return she has had a surgical operation and has spent some time in a hospital in southern California. She is now, we trust, on the way to full recovery and is looking forward with joyous expectation to her return to Africa some time next year.

Carroll and Mrs. Rosa D. Hunter Smith

Carroll Smith and Miss Rosa D. Hunter (whom he afterward married) were accepted by the Board and appointed to Africa. They left New York for that field of labor, in company with other missionaries, April 4, 1902, and arrived at Durban, South Africa, May 20. Brother Smith was one of a family of thirteen children and was converted at the age of twenty-two. Just before receiving the experience of entire sanctification the Lord called him to the foreign field. He spent four and a half years in our seminary at Evansville, Wisconsin. While in Africa, previous to his marriage, he labored at Inhambane, East Africa, and Germiston in the Transvaal. Miss Hunter was converted at the age of thirteen and later was graduated from the Tionesta school in Pennsylvania. Not long after this she heard a definite call to Africa as a missionary and responded, but kept it secret for some time. She was graduated from the State Normal school at Clarion, Pennsylvania, in the fall of 1907. She afterward taught school two years in Pennsylvania and one year in the A. M. Chesbrough Seminary at North Chili, New York. Her last work in Africa was teaching in the Girls' Home School at Fair View. On March 25, 1903, she was united in marriage with Carroll Smith. Because of the death of Brother Agnew, and Mrs. Agnew's return to America on furlough, they at once went to the station at Germiston, Transvaal, and took charge of the work there. Later they spent several years at Greenville Mission Station, Pondoland, where they carried on a successful school in connection with the regular work of the station. Brother Smith was again appointed to Inhambane, and while there had a severe attack of black-water fever. This made it necessary for him to return to the home land. Mrs. Smith also had attacks of fever and at one time the life of their baby girl was despaired of; but the Lord saw fit to bring them safely home, where they arrived in June, 1910, with their two little girls, after having toiled eight years in Africa.

They labored faithfully on the field and are now zealously aiding the work at home. They feel their hearts especially drawn toward the imperative needs of the work at Inhambane. Brother Smith had charge of the work on the Inland district of the South Africa Mission conference as district elder for one year—1907-'08. His health is improving since their return to America.

Nathanael B. and Martha S. Harris Smith

Nathanael B. Smith and wife sailed for Africa, April 4, 1902. They labored faithfully on the field until 1905, when, because of his failing health, it became necessary for them to return home. Soon after their return they resigned their relations to the Board. Brother Smith is now laboring acceptably as pastor in the Susquehanna conference.

J. W. and Jennie Hamilton Haley

J. W. Haley was accepted by the Missionary Board in March, 1902, leaving New York for Africa, April 9, of that year. He was born in Ontario, Canada, where he spent most of his time until leaving for Africa. In the home land he acted as Sunday-school superintendent, labored as exhorter and local preacher, and at the time he was accepted as a missionary was on trial in the West Canada conference. When he went out he overtook the party at London, which left New York April 5, and continued his journey with them. His principal field of labor has been Inhambane, South East Africa.

Jennie Hamilton, who had previously been accepted by the Board, embarked for Africa, January 7, 1905. She is the daughter of one of our preachers in the West Ontario conference. A few months after her arrival she was united in marriage to J. W. Haley, and has been his faithful helpmeet in the work of the Master. At one time she took an inland trip with her husband and baby girl from their station at Inhambane, a distance of 200 miles, traveling through a region where a white woman had never before been seen. She proved her love and devotion to the work at Inhambane by leaving her baby for several months to the care of another missionary in a more healthful climate, while she remained with her husband at that place. The years of labor, mostly in the unhealthful climate at Inhambane, so impaired the health of Brother Haley that it became necessary for him to return to America, and they arrived in New York, April 3, 1909. For some time they have been living on the prairie in Saskatchewan, and his health is much improved. It is hoped that they can return to the work at Inhambane where his success as an organizer and in securing and raising up evangelists and opening and carrying on work among the children has been remarkable.

Dr. W. A. and Mrs. Mary E. Stillson Backenstoe

Dr. W. A. Backenstoe was accepted by the Missionary Board in June, 1903, and left New York for Africa the following November. He was accompanied by his wife, Mary E. Stillson Backenstoe, to whom he was married a short time previous to going out. Sister Backenstoe did not go out under the Board, but was accepted by it October 18, 1904, while on the field. Previous to her acceptance she labored zealously with him in the work. She was graduated from a school in Windsor, New York, and following this taught school. She then took a training class course and the next year attended A. M. Chesbrough Seminary. At the time of conversion she felt that she must be a missionary. When it was fully settled and she was willing to go to Africa, she saw a group of black people around her and an angel above holding out a crown to her. Dr. Backenstoe was graduated from the Latin Scientific college preparatory course at Greenville, Illinois. He afterward took a four years' course at the Medico-chirurgical College at Philadelphia, Pennsylvania, and was licensed to practise in that State. Following his graduation, for one year he was resident physician in the Robert Packer Hospital at Sayre, Pennsylvania. He then took special courses in the hospitals at Philadelphia and New York, and when at home assisted his brother in private practise in Emaus, Pennsylvania. He went out as a medical missionary, and although not having full liberty to do medical work, his reports show that he rendered much needed professional service and also adapted himself to varied circumstances and conditions in connection with the work. His wife has proved an efficient helper, and their influence and work have not only been helpful to our mission, but his professional services have been highly appreciated by natives, and by Colonists outside of our missionaries in Africa. Missionaries and Colonists, as well as natives, were sorry to have them leave, but this was necessary on account of her poor health. They are now on their way to the home land, where they expect to arrive before the first of June, 1911.

Jules and Elizabeth Ellen Ryff

Jules Ryff and wife were accepted by the Board, June 15, 1903, and appointed to go out to Africa as soon as there should be sufficient funds. They left New York for Africa in the early part of February, 1904. He spent four years at Settle Seminary, where he was graduated in 1900. The next year was spent in teaching in Seattle Seminary and in studying the elementary branches of the Medical Course at the Washington State University. Brother Ryff was born in Switzerland and came to America when sixteen years of age, being called to the foreign work in March, 1895. Mrs. Ryff was converted at the age of thirteen and united with the Free Methodist church. Four years afterward she received the experience of entire sanctification and was called to the work of a foreign missionary. She attended school at Seattle Seminary parts of four years. Both had a persuasion that their field of labor was in India; but when the door was open for them to go to Africa, they accepted it as a call of the Lord and have been laboring there, the most of the time at Germiston, Johannesburg, South Africa. He has filled the office of district elder for one year, and has been acting president of the conference for one year. He was its secretary for a year or two previous. Their labors are highly appreciated by their co-workers and by others outside of our mission.

Miss Nellie Reed

Miss Reed was accepted by the Directors of the General Missionary Board, March 29, 1904, and appointed to go out to Africa as soon as funds were sufficient. She embarked at New York for Africa, January 7, 1905. Miss Reed was born at Little Sandusky, Minnesota. There she attended the public schools and later went to Wessington Springs Seminary, South Dakota, where she took a four years' course and was graduated in 1894. She afterward taught school at different places with great success. Later she took a normal course at Huron College, South Dakota, receiving a Teacher's State Certificate from that institution. The year 1896 was spent by her in Chicago, attending the Free Kindergarten of Armour Institute. While in Chicago she did some mission work, visiting among the poor, and was one of several who sang at the Mary Thompson Hospital Sunday afternoons and also did work at the police stations. Later she taught in our seminary at Seattle, Washington, and while there spent one evening in the week giving instruction in a school for the Chinese. Her call to foreign missionary work in Africa was very clear and satisfactory, and, although prominent fields of usefulness were open for her in the home land, she felt clearly persuaded that she should not accept them, but follow her God-given conviction in regard to foreign work. The most of her time since reaching Africa has been spent in teaching in the Girls' School and Home at Fair View, being associated with Miss Allen in that work.

The Junior Missionary work originated in connection with the out-going of Miss Reed, and she was the first missionary to be supported by funds raised by the Juniors. The work of the Juniors has been very encouraging. From the first they have given more than enough to support Miss Reed, and later their funds have increased so that several missionaries have been supported by them. Miss Reed's interesting letters to the Juniors have helped to increase their interest.

A. E. and Matilda Deyo Haley

A. E. Haley was accepted by the Directors of the General Missionary Board at their meeting, October 18, 1904, and was appointed by them to go out to Africa. At another meeting of the Directors held November 17 of that year the Secretary was requested to arrange to send him out to Africa immediately. Accordingly he embarked at New York, January 7, 1905. Miss Deyo was accepted by the Board, October 12, 1905, and appointed to Africa. She left for that field of labor, December 8, 1906. Permission was given by the General Missionary Board, at a meeting held at Greenville, Illinois, June 15, 1907, for A. E. Haley and Miss Matilda Deyo to marry, which they did soon after. They have labored in Natal the most of the time until recently, but at the South Africa Mission conference, held in the spring of 1910, they were appointed to Germiston (Johannesburg), South Africa, where they have since been laboring. At present he is secretary of the conference. The previous year he was both secretary and treasurer.

Rev. and Mrs. A. D. Warren

Rev. A. D. Warren and wife, of the East Michigan conference, were accepted by the Board, October 18, 1904, and appointed to go out to Africa. At a meeting of the Directors held July 19, 1905, the Board took the following action in relation to their going out: "On motion, the Missionary Secretary was instructed to write A. D. Warren and wife that, in view of the precarious condition of Mrs. Warren's health, and the condition of our treasury, it has been thought best to discontinue their relation to the Board." Sister Warren died not long after this, and he has not been reappointed by the Board.

W. S. and Mrs. Annie Davis Woods

Mr. W. S. Woods and wife were accepted by the Board, October 11, 1905, and appointed to go out to Africa. They embarked at New York for that field, December 16, 1905.

Brother Woods was born in the State of Colorado, where he
continued to live for thirty-six years. At the second Free
Methodist meeting he ever attended he was converted. Later
he attended Orleans Seminary, Nebraska. Sister Woods was
of Swedish parentage. A large portion of her life, previous to
going to Africa, was spent in Colorado, where she attended the public schools. She was converted under the labors of Rev. C. W. Stamp, in a meeting held at Canon City.
The Lord gave her a missionary spirit and she embraced opportunities for seeking the lost. She often called on her
neighbors and prayed with them. They were married in 1892.
They offered themselves to the Board in response to a call for
a man and wife to look after the interests of the Fair View
land, or farm. They have labored diligently on temporal lines
of work, and have also aided our other missionaries in the
spiritual part of the work. Their labors in both respects have
been appreciated and helpful. He has done much hard work
on the farm. His last reports are very encouraging and show
that his work has not been in vain.

Miss Maggie La Barr

Miss LaBarr was accepted by the Board, October 13, 1906,
and appointed to go out to Africa. She left New York for
that field, December 8, 1906. She was born in Isabella county, Michigan. At the age of eleven years she attended a camp-
meeting and sought and received the witness of pardon. About
that time she joined the Free Methodist church. At the age
of fourteen she felt a definite call to the foreign field, and at
the same time her mother felt that this was to be her work
and consecrated her to it. She attended Ferris Institute at
Big Rapids, Michigan, and prepared herself for teaching. She
spent about eight years in the school room, after which she
went to Olive Branch Mission, Chicago, and spent some time
in assisting in the work at that mission, immediately preceding her out-going to Africa. Since her arrival in Africa she
has taught both in the Girls' School at Fair View, and in the
training school at Edwaleni, and has also spent some time in
evangelistic work.

George Donald Schlosser

George D. Schlosser was accepted and appointed as a missionary to Africa, and went out, December 8, 1906. He remained there for about two years when, feeling strongly persuaded, according to previous convictions, that his field of labor was China, and receiving permission from the Board to go there at his own expense, he left Africa for that field in 1908.

Clyde Curtis Foreman

Clyde Curtis Foreman, of Tionesta, Pennsylvania, applied to the Board for an appointment to labor at Inhambane, East Africa. He was accepted by the Directors in October, 1906, and appointed to go to Lisbon, Portugal, to study the Portuguese language, preparatory to going to Inhambane. Mr. Foreman was twenty-one years of age at this time. He left New York the middle of March, 1907, and arrived at Lisbon the 3rd of April. He stayed about two weeks, when he returned to the home land. He worked at his employment as civil engineer and repaid to the Board the amount of money for his going out. At that time the Board encouraged him that if he still felt that he was called to Inhambane, after having had more experience, they would again consider his case. He applied and was accepted the second time in October, 1908, and left New York City, April 17, 1909, going direct to Lisbon, Portugal. There he labored zealously in the study of the language for about two months; but the climate was very hot, and in spite of his brave struggle to endure it, the heat so affected his head that he could not study or sleep and it became necessary for him to return to America, which he did, arriving in New York, October 11, 1909.

Ole Kragerud

Ole Kragerud was accepted by the General Missionary Board in 1907 and appointed to labor at Germiston, Johannesburg, South Africa. Previous to his being accepted by the

Board he had assisted our missionaries in the work at Germiston. This he continued to do until the spring of 1910, when he received an appointment from the South Africa Mission conference to assist Rev. N. B. Ghormley in the school work at Edwaleni, where he is now laboring. He is a Norwegian by birth, but has acquired sufficient knowledge of the English language to be able to use it quite successfully. He has studied Zulu and can use that language fairly well. He took a three years' course in a technical school in Christiana, Norway, and received a certificate showing that his standing was good in his studies. He has labored acceptably and efficiently.

Rev. and Mrs. Newton Baxter Ghormley

Rev. and Mrs. Ghormley were accepted by the Board, June 17, 1907, and appointed to labor in Natal, South Africa. They left New York for their field, November 2, 1907. Brother Ghormley was born near Yates City, Illinois, and removed with his parents to Iowa when nine years of age. Later he lived in South Dakota, where he was converted at the age of twenty-one and was sanctified wholly two weeks later. He began to preach about the year 1870. He was educated in the public schools, at Wessington Springs Seminary, and Greenville College. He was engaged as teacher in Wessington Springs Seminary, in Evansville and Los Angeles Seminaries, and was principal at Orleans Seminary for four years. He served as circuit preacher in Dakota and Wisconsin, was ordained deacon by General Superintendent Coleman, and elder by General Superintendent Jones. He was married to Rachel Josephine Baird, August 10, 1896. Three children, Glen Erwin, Verne Gordon and Dale Norman, accompanied them to Africa. In his youth Brother Ghormley was trained by his parents after the style of strict old-school Presbyterianism. He attributes his usefulness, in part, under God, to early training in the Scriptures. The Board gave him charge of the Training School for young men at Edwaleni, Natal, South Africa.

Since reaching the field Brother Ghormley has been in charge of that school and has labored diligently and efficiently, not only in educating and training the native young men for teaching and evangelistic work, but has also spent much time in preparing the station at Edwaleni for school buildings, and for a permanent place for all of our work connected with the school and mission station there. A number of buildings have been erected since he took charge of the work, probably the most important ones being a dwelling house for himself and family, and a building which is used for the accommodation of the school proper. Larger accommodations are needed for the school, and it is hoped they may be provided ere long. Mrs. Ghormley has ably assisted him in the work.

Miss Ethel A. Cook

Miss Cook was accepted by the Directors of the General Missionary Board, March 20, 1907, and appointed to go out to Natal, South Africa. She left New York, November 2, 1907. She labored part of the time in Natal, spent a little time in Pondoland, and the remainder of her time was spent at Inhambane, East Africa. Because of impaired health it became imperatively necessary for her to return to the home land, which she did, arriving in New York, April 3, 1909. Sister Cook was highly appreciated by her co-workers while in Africa, and it was with great reluctance that she left the field. Her departure for home was felt to be a great loss to our work and workers there. Since her return she has been gradually improving and at the present time her health is quite good.

Rev. G. G. and Mrs. Hattie L. Flenniken Kessel

Rev. G. G. Kessel and wife were accepted as missionaries by the Board, June 18, 1907, and appointed to go out to Africa in company with Rev. and Mrs. N. B. Ghormley. Brother Kessel was born June 28, 1868, and Mrs. Kessel was born March 25, 1871. They were residents of Kansas the most of the time previous to their being accepted as missionaries. His education was received in the district school, in Orleans Seminary, Orleans, Nebraska, and in Willamette University of Salem, Oregon. He taught several terms of school. He was received on trial in the West Kansas conference in 1892, and continued to act as pastor in that conference until 1900, when he was elected district elder, which office he held for four years. He was transferred to the California conference in 1904, and was elected district elder of the whole California conference for one year. After this, in 1906-'07, he was pastor at San Jose, California. Mrs. Kessel was educated in the grammar and high schools of Osborne, Kansas, and at Orleans Seminary, Nebraska. Brother Kessel was converted November 24, 1884, and Mrs. Kessel in December, 1885.

After their acceptance by the Board, it was found necessary for Mrs. Kessel to have a surgical operation. Because of this their outgoing was delayed and they did not leave New York for Africa until May 2, 1908. Their two children, John and Edward, accompanied them. For the first two years Brother Kessel had charge of the work at Fair View as pastor, and also acted as district elder. The past year he has been acting as pastor at Fair View. His responsibilities in connection with the work of pastor and elder seemed too great for a new missionary unacquainted with the language, but he has applied himself to the study of the language and made encouraging progress. His zeal in grappling with the language, at his age, is very commendable, and should be an inspiration to some who are younger in years. Mrs. Kessel has been his zealous and successful helpmeet, and her labors have been blessed of the Lord.

Rev. August M. and Mrs. Mary E. Damon Anderson

Rev. August M. Anderson and wife were accepted by the Board, June 25, 1907, at Greenville, Illinois, and appointed to go out as soon as the funds would warrant. They embarked for Africa, May 2, 1908, going out with Rev. and Mrs. G. G. Kessel and family. Brother Anderson was born in Skjeberg county, Norway, May 18, 1878, and came to the United States in 1881. His home most of the time since arriving here has been in Minnesota and South Dakota. He joined the Free Methodist church when nineteen years of age, and received a local preacher's license one year from that time. He supplied as pastor one year in the South

Dakota annual conference and attended Wessington Springs Seminary, where he completed the Christian Worker's Course. Later he acted as supply on a charge in the South Dakota conference for two years. From there he went to Greenville College and was in attendance at that school for some time before leaving for Africa. Sister Anderson is the daughter of Rev. C. M. Damon. She was converted at three years of age and received into the church on probation when four years and ten months old. She taught school at different places and was Brother Anderson's assistant as supply on a charge in the South Dakota conference. Her education was obtained at our seminaries in Evansville, Wisconsin and Orleans, Nebraska, and at our college at Greenville, Illinois, where she completed the Bachelor of Pedagogy course. Upon their arrival in Africa, they were appointed to have charge of the Greenville Mission Station, Pondoland, where they have labored until the present time with acceptability. They have been called to pass through some severe tests in connection with her sickness and the death of their child. The cattle disease also has placed severe restrictions upon them. Their zeal in endeavoring to have the work enlarged in connection with their station is commendable, and they have been rewarded with encouraging fruit.

Rev. and Mrs. E. M. Sandys

Rev. E. M. Sandys and wife were received by the Directors at their meeting held October 15, 1907, and appointed to go out to Durban, South Africa, to take charge of a prospective new station to be opened in the city of Durban, the Board to be responsible for their expenses to the field, but not for their maintenance while on the field. As the Board did not purchase property for the prospective new station at Durban, and as at the annual Board meeting held October, 1910, there was no immediate prospect of opening a station there, it discontinued E. M. Sandys and wife as Board missionaries.

Miss Luella Newton

Miss Newton was converted, January 6, 1901, and united with the Free Methodist church the same evening. Her first

call to missionary work was in July, 1901, at a camp-meeting.
For several years she supplied work as pastor in the Oil City
and Pittsburg conferences, and held an evangelist's license.
For three years previous to taking up evangelistic work she
taught school very acceptably. For a short time she was in
comparatively poor health, but in answer to prayer received
renewed strength and with it the conviction that this strength
was given her for labors in Africa. The way soon opened for
her to go out with Rev. and Mrs. G. G. Kessel as instructor of
their two sons. On May 2, 1908, the party left New York,
arriving in Durban, Natal, South Africa, June 14, 1908. For
two years Miss Newton taught John and Edward Kessel and
a part of this time Susie and Harry Agnew. In connection
with teaching she also assisted the missionaries in their work,
and her labors were highly appreciated. Miss Newton was ac
cepted by the Board at their annual meeting held in Chicago,
Illinois, October 19, 1910. Since her acceptance as a Board
missionary she has been successfully laboring with Miss Mag-
gie LaBarr on the Itemba Mission Station, Natal, South Africa.

Frank Millard Long

Frank Millard Long was accepted as a missionary by the
Directors of the General Missionary Board, at a special meeting held in Chicago, Illinois, April 13, 1910, and appointed to
go out to Inhambane, East Africa. He was directed to go to
Lisbon, Portugal, and as soon as possible, after making satisfactory progress in the study of the language there, to go on
to Inhambane, East Africa. At the time of his acceptance
he was acting as secretary of the Young Men's Christian Association, but expected to be released from his engagement
in Association work to go out soon after he was accepted by
the Directors. Not having succeeded in being released from
his engagement, his outgoing has been delayed, but it is expected that he will leave for Lisbon or Africa in August or
September next. He was born in Kansas and later lived with
his parents in the state of Oklahoma. He was graduated at a
high school in that State, and in the fall of 1904 entered the
State University. In 1908 he received the degree of A. B. and

in 1909 the degree of A. M. His educational advantages qualify him for very successful work as an instructor on the foreign field.

Elbert H. and Charlotte E. Johns Wells

Elbert H. Wells and wife were accepted by the Missionary
Board, October 20, 1910, and appointed to labor at Inhambane, Southeast Africa. At that time they were attending
Greenville College, but accepted the appointment and at once
began preparations for the work to which they had been
called by God and the church. They had previously been
graduated from the A. M. Chesbrough Seminary. On January 11, 1911, Brother and Sister Wells sailed from New York
City and reached our mission station in the Transvaal on the
10th of March, after having spent two or three weeks with
the missionaries at Fair View. They are studying the language at Modderfontein, Transvaal, for a few months before
going on to the station at Inhambane.

Sister Wells, formerly Charlotte E. Johns, had been accepted as a missionary to Africa in the fall of 1908, and was
to have been sent out as soon as there was an opening for a
single young woman and funds would warrant.

ASSOCIATE MISSIONARIES

Mr. and Mrs. A. A. Miller

On October 14, 1907, the Missionary Board adopted a report in the case of A. A. Miller and family. The report con-
tained several provisions, according to his request, regarding
his work under the direction of the Board and the superintendent in charge of the work at Inhambane, South Africa, as
an Associate Missionary. He was to go out as Associate Missionary of the Board, the Board not to accept any financial
responsibility for his outgoing, nor for his living expenses
while on the field or when in the home land. It was further
agreed that the Board should provide means to secure a mission station and necessary buildings for A. A. Miller and wife

to work among the Machopi people in the interior, from In hambane, when satisfactory conditions on his part were met, the property thus secured by Board money to be held by the Board, and under its control. Brother Miller embarked for East Africa, January 16, 1909, accompanied by his wife and several children. Previous to his acceptance by our Board he had been associated for some time with our missionaries at Inhambane and in South Africa in missionary work. Since his return he has labored the most of the time at Inhambane, looking after our work under the direction of the missionary in charge at that place. He has also made a tour into the interior among the Machopis and selected a site for a mission station among that people, where he hopes to labor in the future. The Machopis are recognized as Peter Maguheni's people.

Dr. Harriet E. Sheldon

Miss Sheldon made application to go out to Africa as a Board missionary; but fearing that she would not be able to do the required work of a missionary on the field because of her age and other conditions, the Woman's Board did not recommend her as a candidate to the General Missionary Board. The Board, however, considered her case and referred it to the Board of Directors without taking further action. At a meeting of the Directors held January 5, 1909, they approved of her going out to East Africa as an Associate Missionary with A. A. Miller and wife. The Directors also appropriated $200 for her outgoing expenses from money raised for the Machopi people, among whom she expected to do her work. Miss Sheldon sailed from New York City, January 16, 1909. When she reached Durban she was in a feeble state of health, and upon learning more about climatic conditions at Inhambane and the adjoining regions, which she did not know when she left America, she decided that her health would not permit of her laboring on the East Coast, so she remained in Natal. For a time she rendered Mrs. Lillie A. Agnew valuable assistance, both in evangelistic work and on her station at Magog, and as teacher for her children. As our Board had not accepted Miss Sheldon as a regular missionary and had made no provision for her salary, and as she was not able physically to engage in the work under Brother Miller as at first planned, therefore, she thought best to leave our work altogether and became associated with the "Sent of God" people at Beulah Mission in Natal, where there was an encouraging opening for her. Miss Sheldon is still at heart with the church of her choice, for which she spent many years of faithful toil in mission work in the home land and as an evangelist before going to Africa.

Miss Myrta Smith

Miss Myrta Smith, of Franklin, Pennsylvania, made application to be sent out to Africa with J. P. Brodhead and family when they returned after having their furlough. She offered to pay her own expenses to the field and to be at no expense to the Board after arriving in South Africa. The Woman's Auxiliary Board considered her case carefully and recommended her as a favorable candidate to the General Missionary Board. At a meeting of the Board in the fall of 1909 they passed a resolution recommending Miss Smith as a suitable person to be sent out as an Associate Missionary to labor with Mr. and Mrs. Brodhead under the direction of the South Africa Mission conference, the Board to accept of no financial obligations in her case. This recommendation was accepted by the Board of Directors, October 21, 1909. Miss Smith embarked at New York City for Durban, South Africa, with Brother and Sister Brodhead and their two daughters, November 21, 1909. She has since been doing acceptable work at the new station in Pondoland, known as Critchlow Mission, and writes that she praises the Lord for the privilege of having a share in giving the light of the gospel to those needy people in Pondoland.

Faith Missionaries

These missionaries did not go out by direct appointment of the General Missionary Board or of the Pentecost Bands.

Robert L. Harris, of the Texas conference, embarked for Africa at New York, November 17, 1885, being twenty-four years of age at that time. He went to Liberia on the West Coast. Rev. C. B. Ebey, writing concerning his work in Africa, said that God gave him souls for his ministry, and he explored up and down a number of rivers in Liberia. He arrived in New York on his way back from Africa, Sunday, May 23, 1886. He embarked for Africa the second time with a party of several others, October 30, 1886, and arrived in Africa, December 15. He remained in Africa until April 15, 1887, and then returned to America for another band of missionaries, arriving in Chicago about the middle of May. Soon after his return he made a call for money to purchase a ship for the purpose of transporting missionaries to Liberia. He also wrote a small book on his work and about the workers who went out to Africa with him. His plans did not meet with the approval of the church, generally, and he never returned to Africa.

Eunice Knapp, Jennie Torrence, and Lizzie Cox went out to Liberia with R. L. Harris on his second trip.

Sister Knapp was a native of Illinois, and was forty-three years of age. She died with fever six weeks after landing.

Jennie Torrence stayed about two years in Liberia, and then returned to America. Lizzie Cox came back at the same time and did not return.

Pentecost Band Missionaries

Jennie Torrence and Mattie North went out to Africa under the Pentecost Bands in October, 1890. They reached Monrovia, December 23 of that year, and began work with G. W. and Mrs. M. W. Chapman. Jennie Torrence died with hemorrhage of the stomach, February 16, 1891.

Mattie E. North died March 23, 1891, of chills and fever. She was from Illinois.

G. W. and Mrs. Mary Weems Chapman left America for Monrovia, September 18, 1889. Charles Sumner Kerwood went to Monrovia with G .W. Chapman. He was taken with African fever in March, 1890, and died on the third of the following September. He went out from the Vanguard training Home, St. Louis.

Rev. V. A. Dake went to Africa to visit the Band workers

soon after the close of his conference—the Illinois—in the fall of 1891. He died January 3, 1892, in Africa. G. W. Chapman and wife returned to America soon after the death of V. A. Dake.

C. H. Westfall and wife went out as Band missionaries in 1886, and returned in 1887. Mrs. Mary Sharp and Bishop Taylor loaned them money for their return trip.

Their return and the deaths of so many of the Pentecost Band and Faith missionaries in Liberia has ,caused these bodies to cease sending missionaries to that field. This field is proverbially known as the grave of the white missionaries.

Statistics—Africa

Missionaries regularly appointed by the Board and sent out......43
Missionaries regularly appointed, but who for various reasons have
    not gone out 8
Missionaries accepted by the Board while on the field............. 4
Associate missionaries accepted by the Board and sent out.......... 4
*"Faith" missionaries gone out................................. 4
*"Pentecost Band" missionaries gone out........................ 8
                                                             —

    Total..71

*These did not go out under the Board.

INDIA

Rev. Ernest F. and Phebe E. Ward

Rev. Ernest F. and Phebe E. Ward, his wife, were the first missionaries who went out to the foreign field from the Free Methodist church, and therefore to them belongs the honor of being the leaders in our missionary work. They arrived in India in January, 1881. They went out as faith missionaries, and to meet expenses used their own means as was necessary.

They labored in Central India, at Burhampur, where he built a mission house, which he sold to William Taylor's South India Mission. Immediately after this they settled at Ellichpur, where they labored for several years and had a number of sieges of malarial fever. While there their labors were principally among the Korkus. Later they decided to change their location again and go farther South, where the languages were less mixed, so they sold the property which they had acquired at Ellichpur to the Jabneel Mission of London. Brother Ward baptized a few persons while living at Ellichpur.

Both Brother and Sister Ward were recognized as missionaries of the church, but at that time, as they felt that God had called them out on the faith line, therefore they could not come under the Board, as by so doing it would appear to the world that they had the Board behind them as a financial backing, and this would reflect on their faith principle, at least in India. While at Burhampur they sold about 5,000 Bible portions and tracts, and while laboring at Ellichpur some 15,000 more. The average size of the tracts sold was equal in size to the book of Romans. Aside from these, they distributed gratuitously tens of thousands of leaflet tracts. The literature they sold and gave away was printed in eleven languages and dialects—Hindi, Urdu, Marathi, Gujerati, Telugu, Tamil, Panjabi, Gondi, Portuguese, Hebrew and English. In some cases they gave Scripture portions free to inquirers. They were privileged to see some encouraging fruit from this work. During the famine they took in orphans and were assisted by Sister Ranf. They gathered native Sunday-schools in four different places where they labored, having as

many as 1,000 on their register a year, but a small attendance
usually. Sisters Ward and Ranf labored especially among
the women. They sat down on the floor in the houses of the
natives and sang, prayed and read out of some simple book
as "Line upon Line," "Peep of Day," and "Marathi First
Book," or would show the "Wordless Book," which has blank
pages of different colors to illustrate sin and the blood of
Christ. Brother Ward speaks of one fair they attended about
fifty miles east of Ellichpur, where there were about 75,000
persons assembled, and they were the only Christians present
to give the word of life. At one village where he was preaching, in 1890, the natives all admitted that it would be just
and right to take the village idol and pitch it into the river,
but no one was willing to act. In traveling up the steep de-
files in the hills the roads were so rough, in some places like
flights of stairs cut in the rock, that they were obliged to take
hold and lift the cart up the steps as the oxen found it impos-
sible to pull through without assistance.

Referring to his labors, Brother Ward says, "In 1889 I
preached in 82 cities and villages, in 1890 in 101, in 1891 in
82 villages." They labored in Central India and remained
on the field until 1892, when they returned to America. Excepting what they used of their own means toward their support, it was principally provided through the Free Methodist
church, as information concerning their work was published
in the *Free Methodist*, and gifts for their aid were sent to the
Missionary Treasurer to be forwarded to them, or were
sent direct. When they went out the General Missionary
Board was not incorporated, as this took place, June 19, 1885.
For some years they considered the Board their advisory committee. They left America again for India in 1893. From the
time of their return until about 1894 they continued to labor
on what they had considered the "faith line" of missionary
work, that is they had the work brought before the people in
certain publications, and gave themselves to prayer that
God would supply all their needs. In 1894 they became associated with our missionaries in work and so continued until October, 1906, when they were accepted by the Board.
Since then they have labored very satisfactorily with our missionaries.

As Sister Ward had been very ill and was weak in body, and Brother Ward was in great need of rest and change of climate, they returned again to America, arriving in New York in May, 1910. Their three daughters had previously come to America and were attending school at Seattle Seminary, Washington. Upon their arrival Brother and Sister Ward proceeded to the Coast as soon as possible and arrived there in time to see their oldest daughter, Ethel, graduated. They attended camp-meetings and held missionary services as they were able up to the time of Sister Ward's death, which occurred September 1, 1910, after a short illness.

Brother Ward has labored faithfully in holding meetings in the interest of the work in India during the past winter and spring, and his labors have been very successful. The Lord has given him many years of service on the foreign field. His work there has been largely evangelistic. His success in acquiring the languages in India has been good. The Lord has especially preserved him in health, and though he has spent many years in that hot and trying climate, he is still quite vigorous and strong. Very good success has been given him on temporal lines of work, especially in having charge of the erection of buildings for the missionary work. He is looking forward with hope to the time, in the near future, when he shall return to India, and may be accompanied by his oldest daughter, Miss Ethel.

Mary Louisa Ranf and Miss Julia Zimmerman

Mary Louisa Ranf and Miss Julia Zimmerman were accepted by the executive committee of the General Missionary Board in November or December of 1885, to go out to India to assist Ernest and Phebe Ward. They left New York for India, December 17, 1885. Miss Zimmerman left the work June 12, 1886, and engaged in zenana work, and did not return to our work. Later she was discontinued as a Board missionary.

Miss Ranf continued to be associated with Brother and Sister Ward in labors at Burhampur, India, until her tragic death which occurred November 6, 1890. It was caused by knocking a lamp, which was insecurely fastened, from its position; the lamp breaking, the oil went on her clothes and caught fire. All of the clothes were burned from her body except her shoes. She lived only about five and a half hours.

Mrs. Celia J. Ferries McMurry

Celia J. Ferries left Chicago, Illinois, for India in February, 1891. She was born in Portsmouth, England, and came with her parents to America in May, 1869. About 1874 her parents united with the Free Methodist church. She was converted at the age of ten years, and four years later received her special impression for the foreign missionary work. Later she spent four years at Evansville Seminary and was graduated from that institution June 8, 1887. In February, 1888, she fully settled it to follow her convictions in regard to going to the foreign field. Her heart was especially drawn out toward the women of India. Her brother has been a preacher in the Illinois conference for many years. For five and one-half years she remained in India, and the most of that time acted as superintendent of the work. She secured our station at Yeotmal, India. Her assistants were Anna Jones and Mattie J. Miller. She left Bombay, India, August 21, 1896, for a furlough home, and arrived at New York the 16th or 17th of September. On October 23, 1897, she left New York the second time for India.

V. G. McMurry was accepted by the Board and left New York for India, October 23, 1897. He married Miss Ferries in the spring or summer of 1898. At a meeting of the General Missionary Board, October 17, 1900, provision was made for his ordination by a Methodist missionary bishop in India, and he was ordained. He was appointed by the Board, at its annual meeting in 1901, as superintendent of the mission at Yeotmal, and again at the annual meeting in 1902 to continue this relation to the mission until the session of the general conference the following June. At a meeting of the Missionary Board held in connection with the general conference, June, 1903, action was taken approving of the return of V. G. and Mrs. McMurry to the home land, as soon as, in the judgment of the secretary, it was thought best. They came back to America, arriving the latter part of 1903, and spent some

time laboring in public meetings in the interest of missionary
work.

At the annual meeting of the Missionary Board, October,
1904, V. G. McMurry and wife, having tendered their resignations to the Board, and arranged to go out to India under
the auspices of the Methodist Episcopal church, the Directors
accepted their resignations.

They are still in India, laboring under the Methodist Episcopal Board.

Miss Anna Jones

Miss Jones, having been accepted by the Board, went out
to India, arriving there September 3, 1892. She remained in
India about four and a half years. Much of the time while on
the field her health was poor and she returned home in April
or May of 1907. As the Board did not think best for her to
return, her relation was discontinued.

Mrs. Emma Appling Gilpatrick

Emma Appling went out to India under the Pentecost
Bands, December 13, 1893, and arrived at Bombay, India, January 20, 1894. She labored with them the most of the time
until accepted on trial by the Missionary Board, September
3, 1895. She was received in full relation, October, 1896.
Her health failed and she was advised by a physician
and by our missionaries on the field to return home. She did
so, arriving here in December, 1900. Her labors under the
Board were mostly evangelistic, excepting a year and a half
when she had charge of the Girls' Orphanage. Her health
gradually improved, so that in the spring of 1901 she was
able to go out nursing, and the latter part of the summer
and in the fall to attend conferences. The latter part of October she commenced to take a course in a hospital with a
view to going back to India. Her health failed because of ex-
posure and taking cold, and for a time grave fears of her recovery were entertained. Later, in answer to prayer, her
health was restored and she labored successfully on a charge
in the Central Illinois conference for some time. At a meet-

ing of the Board held at Greenville, Illinois, June 15, 1903, in
connection with the general conference, her case was pre-
sented to the Board and she was accepted and appointed to go
out again to India. She spent some time laboring in public
meetings in the interests of our foreign work, before leaving
New York for India, October 23, 1903. She labored ef
fectually in India for some time, but her health again became impaired to the extent that it was thought best for her
to return to America, which she did in June, 1907. Since her
return her health has not been fully restored. February 4,
1910, she was married to Mr. Thomas Herbert Gilpatrick, of
Seattle, Washington. It is not expected that she will return
to the foreign field.

Miss Mattie J. Miller

Miss Miller was accepted by the Board for India, October
17, 1894, and embarked for that field soon after, arriving at
Bombay in December following. She labored for about six
years in India, being associated with Miss Ferries and Miss
Jones in the work at Yeotmal. She returned to America
early in January, 1900. Her resignation was tendered to the
Board the following October, and was accepted.

Rev. H. L. and Abbie Crockett

Rev. H. L. Crockett and wife, having been accepted by the
Board, left New York for India, with their daughter, Vangie,
October 23, 1897. They remained about three years. Brother
Crockett stood the climate wall, and was abundant in labors
while on the field. Sister Crockett's health of mind and body
failed, and from being a healthy woman, whose weight was
about two hundred pounds when she went out, she was
reduced to eighty or ninety pounds at the time of her return
to America in the fall of 1900. The physician in India gave
her no hope of recovery if she remained in that country, so
very reluctantly they came back to America. On their way it
was feared she would not live to see the home land. However, the Lord preserved her, and after her return, by the
blessing of God and a change of climate, her health was much

improved. It was not thought wise, because of her condition of health, to have them return to India, and they sent in their resignations to the Board, which were accepted in October, 1901. Brother Crockett resumed his work as an itinerant preacher in the Susquehanna conference of the church, where he has since labored as pastor and district elder.

Rev. and Mrs. J. T. Taylor

Rev. and Mrs. J. T. Taylor, having been accepted by the Board, left New York for India, January 19, 1901. Brother Taylor was born in Ireland, March 23, 1860. He attended country school until he was about sixteen years of age, when his parents sent him to Belfast, Ireland, to be employed as an apprentice in a wholesale dry goods business house. His parents were Presbyterians and brought him up to conscientiously regard the commandments of the Lord, especially the keeping of the Sabbath day. While at Belfast, away from home influences and restraints, he drifted from his home instructions. A Christian young man came to the same store where he was apprenticed and was associated with him in labors. Through his influence Brother Taylor was brought under conviction and sought and found forgiveness of sins.

In May, 1881, he left Ireland for America and arrived at Evanston, Illinois, the first of June. Soon after this he attended meetings held by Revs. Hanmer, Hanna and Kelsey. He sought the Lord anew and united with the Free Methodist church at Evanston in 1882. He received the experience of entire sanctification in 1886. In the fall of 1887 he was received into the Illinois annual conference of the Free Methodist church as a traveling preacher on probation. From then until January, 1901, he was in the active work in this conference, his circuits being Peoria and Pekin, Winnebago and Ridott, Fairbury and Weston, Peoria and Limestone. From 1895 to 1897 he was district elder of the Fox and Rock River districts, then pastor at Aurora, Humboldt Park (Chicago), and at Dearborn street (Chicago) about three months. He resigned his work at the last named place to go to India. He was married to Miss Sarah Behner, of Peoria, in 1889. She was taken from him to her heavenly reward in 1899. In the fall of 1900 he was married to Miss Margaret E. Fallon, of Peoria, Illinois. Immediately upon arriving in India he commenced a diligent study of the Marathi language and has been able to use it successfully in his labors among the natives. He was secretary of the mission in India in 1901-'02, and in 1903 was appointed superintendent of our work in India by the General Missionary Board. He was reappointed to this office until his return to America in 1907. He also acted as treasurer a part of the time before his return. His labors in India were principally evangelistic.

Sister Taylor was born in Peoria county, Illinois, and was educated in the public schools, spending a year and a half in high school. She was more or less associated with our people from her youth, and at a Free Methodist camp meeting held in Elgin, Illinois, August 16, 1899, she was brought out into the light of God's salvation. Having felt that the Lord would have her serve Him in India as a missionary, when the call came for Brother Taylor to go out to that field, she was quite in accord with him in responding to the same. They were of one heart and mind to offer themselves for work in that far-away land, and their interest has not abated with the experiences they have had on that field. The serious condition of her health was the special reason of their return in 1907. Her health improved while in the home land and as a physician expressed the opinion that she might, by being careful, get along as well in India as in America, they returned, November 3, 1908. Her health has been poor since going back and it is feared she will not long be able to continue on the field. Since their return to India Brother Taylor has acted as superintendent and treasurer of the mission, and his labors have been very helpful to the work.

Miss Rose Cox

Miss Cox was accepted by the Board and left for India, January 19, 1901. Her home was in Indiana, where she labored some as an evangelist before going out. She labored zealously in India from the time of her arrival until 1905, when, because of a failure in health, she was returned

to the home land in the spring of that year. Her health soon
improved and she spent considerable time in speaking in the
interests of our missionary work in India with good success.
It was feared that the condition of her health would not permit of her being returned, but it so improved that the Board
consented for her to go back, which she did November 2, 1907.
She has been laboring on the field there with zeal and faithfulness, her labors being largely evangelistic.

Miss Effie Southworth

Miss Southworth, having been accepted by the Board, left
New York for India, January 19, 1901, in company with
Brother and Sister Taylor and Sister Cox. Miss Southworth
was born at Frankfort Center, New York, August 23, 1874.
Her father was then a member of the Susquehanna conference
of the Free Methodist church, later of the New York, and now
of the Kansas conference. She was converted in January,
1888, and soon united with the Free Methodist church.
She was educated in the graded schools and at Spottsyl-
vania and A. M. Chesbrough seminaries. While attending the A. M. Chesbrough Seminary, in 1897, she was
brought into the experience of perfect love. Later she went
to Kansas and assisted in evangelistic services. With joyful
ness she accepted the appointment for India and has labored
on that field with acceptability and success. She has acquired the language in India, and the most of the time has
had charge of or been connected with the Girls' Orphanage.
Because of the effect of the climate upon her health, it was
thought necessary for her to return to America, and she left
India, June 20, 1908, in company with Rev. M. C. Clarke and
wife. Her physical condition necessitated a surgical operation which, though testing, proved very helpful, and following
this she was stronger and spent some time in public labors
in the interest of our work in India. She returned to that
field in May, 1910, attending the World Missionary Conference at Edinburgh, Scotland, on the way. She spent some time
in England, and then continued her journey to India, arriving there the latter part of August, 1910. She is now actively engaged in the work at the Girls' Orphanage, Yeotmal,
India.

Rev. Mortimer C. and Ethel S. Clarke

Rev. M. C. Clarke and wife were accepted by the Board and left New York for India, September 4, 1901. When accepted by the Board they were living in the state of Washington and were teachers in Seattle Seminary. While in India he acted as treasurer of the mission part of the time, but his principal work was in connection with the Boys' Orphanage. Mrs. Clarke was a faithful helpmeet in that work. Under his labors and guidance the work among the boys went on very successfully, especially the industrial part. Evidently he was adapted to this kind of work, and brought it to such a measure of success that it attracted the attention of many of the Hindu people and helped our influence among them. Because of Sister Clarke's impaired health, they returned to America, leaving India, June 20, 1908. Since their return they have spent some time in public labors, especially in the interest of our work in India. Her health is somewhat improved, but not fully restored, and because of this and the condition of her parents, they are still in the home land. He is now acting with acceptability as pastor of our church at Everett, Washington. It is hoped that they will soon be able to return to India.

Miss Mary E. Chynoweth

Miss Chynoweth was born in West Fairlee, Vermont, February 11, 1873. She was converted at the age of thirteen years, and in the fall of 1899 experienced full salvation. She began teaching in the public schools in Vermont when fifteen years old and from that time for a number of years taught and attended school. She was graduated from the Vermont Methodist Seminary in June, 1895. Following her graduation she took a course in nursing, and in the fall of 1895 entered the Mary Fletcher Hospital in Burlington, Vermont. Her health not being sufficient for the arduous labors in connection with the course at the hospital, she took up private nursing, and later became head nurse in a private sanitarium in Burlington. She remained there for some time, after which she acted as pastor (supply) on a charge in the Susquehanna conference and joined the Free Methodist church, feeling she had found the people of her choice. For about four years she did pastoral work previous to going out to India. Having been accepted by the Board, she left New York for India, January 4, 1902. Being a young woman of good ability, and having had fair opportunities for education in the home land, she succeeded well in acquiring the language and labored princi pally as an evangelist, also assisting in the Girls' Orphanage. While on an evangelistic tour in India, she was taken down with that dreadful disease, smallpox, which proved to be of the virulent type. She was tenderly cared for by Sisters Cox and Southworth, and all the medical skill available was secured, but the disease did its work quickly and she was taken from labor and suffering to her heavenly reward, Jan uary 29, 1908. She has left a record of faithfulness and an influence which will continue to bless others.

Miss Augusta G. Reed

Miss Reed, of Brooklyn, New York, was accepted by the Board, October 16, 1902, and appointed to go out to India as soon as funds would permit. She was continued as an ap pointee for India under the Board until October 19, 1910, when her relation was discontinued. Miss Reed is a thorough ly trained nurse and had spent years in her profession before she was accepted by the Board for India. Immediately pre ceding her acceptance, she spent some time as a nurse in the employment of our government in the Philippines. She greatly desired to return to the Philippine Islands and do missionary work among the people there, so was some what reluctant about going out to India. Evidently these are the special reasons why her going to India was delayed and her relation to the Board finally discontinued.

Samuel D. and Jessie Lively Casberg

Samuel D. Casberg was born in the town of Holmen, Wis consin. His mother died when he was but two weeks old, and five years afterward he was adopted by a family who treated him as their own child and gave him very helpful re ligious instruction. He was converted at the age of fourteen

years, and later entered Seattle Seminary as a student, where
he became acquainted with the Free Methodist people. Having lost his Christian experience, he soon sought the Lord
anew, and the joy of salvation was restored. A short time
afterward he received the experience of entire sanctification.
After spending several years in preparation work at Seattle
Seminary, he was accepted by the 'Board and appointed to go
out to India, leaving New York, January 7, 1906. After laboring about two years in India he was married to Miss Jes-
sie W. Lively. She was born near Wichita, Kansas, and with
her parents lived in that state until she was about twelve
years of age, when they moved to Arizona. She was taught
to fear the Lord in her youth, as her parents were members
of the Presbyterian church. For some years she lived with
her parents on the farm in Arizona. In 1903 she entered the seminary at Seattle as a student. Her first sav-
ing acquaintance with the Savior was when about ten years
of age. She did not retain her Christian experience long, but
when fourteen years of age it was renewed, and later she received the experience of full salvation. While reading the
Christian Herald her attention was called to the condition of
the people in India, and the Lord spoke to her about giving
her life for service to that people. Her attendance at the seminary proved a great blessing, and while there she was more
fully enlightened in regard to the precious doctrines of the
Word of God and became more established in the faith. Three
years were spent at the seminary, and then having applied to
the General Missionary Board to be sent out to India, she
was accepted, and embarked at New York, December 4, 1906,
for that field. She gave herself diligently to the study of the
language upon her arrival at Yeotmal and has been successful in acquiring the same. She has occupied different spheres
of labor on the mission field. Since her marriage to Brother
Casberg, they have been one year in charge of the Boys' Orphanage and Industrial School. Previous to this they were
one year at our new station at Umbri, where he had charge of
building a bungalow for the work. Both Brother and Sister
Casberg have labored diligently and faithfully and the Lord
has preserved them in health. They have one little son.

Rev. G. G. and Mrs. Grace S. Smith Edwards

Rev. G. G. Edwards and wife were accepted by the Board and embarked at New York for India, January 27, 1906. Brother Edwards' father was a preacher in the Free Methodist church for many years, and he was favored with thorough religious instruction in his youth. He was born at Herkimer, New York, and converted when eight years of age. His educational advantages were sufficient to enable him to secure a second grade certificate for teaching school. While teaching he conducted a Sunday-school in the school district where he taught. In the beginning of 1896 he experienced the blessing of entire sanctification. This experience intensified his zeal for the Master and he began to preach the gospel. In 1897 he was married and moved to Seattle, where he attended two terms of school in the seminary, and, being advised by some of the older brethren to take a circuit, he accepted an appointment in the Washington conference where he labored about five years as pastor. When accepted by the Board he was pastor at Buckley, Washington. His first wife died a short time after their marriage. On July 30, 1902, he was married to Miss Grace S. Smith. Sister Smith's father was a traveling preacher in the Free Methodist church, and from childhood she was trained in the church. She was converted at the age of five years, but did not keep this experience. In 1895 she entered our seminary at Seattle, Washington, and on December 5 of that year her religious experience was renewed. A year from that time the Lord called her to the foreign field and she accepted. They have labored on evangelistic lines in India, and for one year have had charge of the Boys' Orphanage and Industrial School. Besides the one child, Herald, who went out with them to India, they have two children born to them on the field. They are now on their way to America.

Miss Gertrude Alcorn

Miss Alcorn was accepted by the Board in 1907. She was born at Heshbon, Pennsylvania. On January 14, 1900, she was converted and called to missionary work. After this she labored about six years in Pentecost Band work and received a definite experience of holiness in June, 1902. At the time of her acceptance by the Board, October 12, 1906, she was in India, having gone out under the Pentecost Bands in November, 1905. She has labored diligently and faithfully in the work in our mission in India and has been successful in acquiring the language.

Miss Mata D. Allee

Miss Allee was accepted by the Board and appointed to India, leaving New York for that field, November 2, 1907. She was born near Saegertown, Pennsylvania. She attended the district school and afterward high school, and began teaching when eighteen years of age. In the fall of 1888 she entered the Edinboro (Pennsylvania) State Normal School. While attending this school she had a fall which injured her seriously, and from the effects of which she did not recover for some years. She had several surgical operations in hope of being restored fully to health. Her religious convictions and views suffered some changes during her illness, which continued for a period of about five years. About September, 1900, she became acquainted with the Free Methodist people and soon after was wonderfully healed in body and received a clear Christian experience. She was definitely called to missionary work in India in August, 1902, while hearing a sermon by Bishop Hogue on the Gerry camp-ground in New York State. She taught in the A. M. Chesbrough Seminary in 1902-03 and took part of the Christian Worker's Course. She has been a teacher in Sunday-schools and acted as superintendent. She spent some time as a student in Greenville College, Illinois.

The climate in India has tested her health severely and she has not been able to do full work as a missionary a large portion of the time since arriving on that field. Because of impaired health and the poor prospect of its being restored at present, she is now on her way home. Her experience and ability, as well as her call, qualify her for successful service in our mission in India, and it is regretted that her condition of health necessitates a return.

Herbert M. and Edna Sherman Damon

Herbert M. Damon and wife were accepted by the Board and appointed to India, leaving New York, November 5, 1909. Brother Damon is a son of Rev. C. M. Damon, whose labors have been largely in the West. Brother Damon was born near Owatona, Minnesota. Later, with his parents he moved to Orleans, Nebraska, where he attended Orleans Seminary for a short time. He was converted about the year 1886. He attended Evansville Seminary, and Whitewater State Normal in Wisconsin. On the 11th of November, 1904, he was fully persuaded that the Lord called him as a foreign missionary and he joined the Student Volunteer Band at Greenville, Illinois. At that time he was attending Greenville College. June 28, 1905, he was married to Miss Edna Sherman, of Greenville, Illinois. Miss Sherman was born not far from Lansing, Michigan, and had the blessing of a Christian home and of faithful religious instruction from her parents. When quite young she was converted. At sixteen years of age she entered high school at Grand Ledge, Michigan, and lost somewhat in her religious experience while attending this school. Later her parents went to Greenville, Illinois. She entered the college as a student and her Christian experience was renewed, which led to her joining the Free Methodist church. October and November of 1903 were spent by her in the Missouri Baptist Sanitarium, in the Nurses' Training Department. She joined the Student Volunteer Band in the spring of 1904, and with others took up the mission study course at the college. After finishing his work at Greenville College, Brother Damon acted as principal of the schools at Cornell, Illinois, for a year. Both he and Mrs. Damon took civil service examinations with the view of teaching in the Philippine Islands, and in August, 1906, were accepted. They sailed from San Francisco, September 14 for the islands, where they spent two and one-half years in teaching under the government. At the end of that time they were offered an opportunity to work in a Christian mission there at an allowance of $1,400 a year, but as there was an opening in the Free Methodist church for them to go out to India, they did not think best to accept the offer of the Christian mission. Having spent the greater part of three years in the tropics, they decided to return to America before commencing work in India, and landed at Seattle on their return trip, June 5, 1909. After spending five months in the States in visiting and recuperating, they embarked for India with their two little girls. The Lord has preserved them in health since their arrival on the field and they have diligently pursued the study of the language with encouraging success.

Miss Edith M. Santee

Miss Santee was accepted by the Board and embarked for India, November 2, 1907. She was graduated at the Niobraso (Nebraska) high school in the year 1899. She was converted in 1901, and in February of 1907 received the experience of full salvation. Soon afterward she united with the Free Methodist church, and through the labors of Sister Rose Cox received a very strong conviction that God would have her labor for Him in India. She attended the general conference of the Free Methodist church held at Greenville, Illinois, in June, 1907. At that time the call was made by the Missionary Board for volunteers for different fields, and she offered herself for work in India and was greatly blessed in so doing. It had been her desire to have more thorough preparation, but feeling that God called her to go out, she accepted the appointment at that time. Diligently and successfully she has pursued the study of the language and has been faithful in her work on the field.

Miss Louise D. Calkins

Miss Calkins was accepted by the Board and embarked for India, November 6, 1909, going with Mr. and Mrs. Herbert M. Damon. She was born at Corning, New York. She was educated in the Corning Academy and later in the Genesee State Normal School, being graduated from each of these institutions. Her conversion took place in the summer of 1897 at a camp-meeting, and July 3, 1904, she united with the Free Methodist church. She received the blessing of holiness, June 27, 1904. In 1903 she began teaching school, and continued in this work until about the time of leaving for India. Her call to India was very definite, so much so that she felt she could not accept an appointment to any other field. For some time her outgoing seemed to be providentially hindered, but later she felt there was a wide open door for her to go and she entered in. Before leaving for the foreign field she assisted some in special evangelistic services. Her success in acquiring the language has been very encouraging and she is laboring faithfully on the field.

Frederick George Mynett

Frederick George Mynett was born May 20, 1884, in Luke's parish, London, and was educated at the St. Giles Cripplegate Boys' School in Fann street, London. He remained in the school until he had passed through all the classes to the highest standard. He was the second best boy in the school and passed the London Bounty Council Labor Test Examination and was allowed to leave school. He was then fourteen years of age. For some years after this he was employed by the Metropolitan Railway Company in London, and was promoted several times while working for them. He spent his leisure time in reading good books from the public library. November 17, 1902, he enlisted as a soldier in the Second Northampton Regiment, which was at that time in Africa. His regiment returned to London in the spring of 1904. While passing a Wesleyan chapel in London, after his return, he felt compelled to go in. While there God spoke to his heart through the minister and he was completely broken up because of his sinful life. He was led to the Savior and received the forgiveness of sins that night, October 1, 1904. On the following February he volunteered again as a soldier and went out to India. There were 1,600 soldiers on the ship with him going out, and he conducted gospel meetings among them. For three years after his arrival he labored zealously among the 1,000 comrades of his regiment to bring them to Christ and was rewarded by seeing several of them converted. He did not acquire the native language at once, but labored among the natives through an interpreter. Referring to his personal work he says: "Every day I found some one to whom I could speak, and they would all listen so attentively, for some of them had never heard of Jesus Christ before, and I felt I must tell every native person I met about Him." Later, while his regiment was at Poona, he took up work among the beggars and outcasts who were found by the roadside. Being granted six weeks leave of duty from his regiment, he spent the most of this time in special prayer that the Lord would clearly show him his work, and he was convinced that God would have him preach the gospel to the native people of India. He wrote to the Wesleyan Missionary Board, offering himself as a worker. A few hours after writing this letter he was introduced to one of our missionaries from Yeotmal, who told him how great was the need for young men workers in the Berar district. He felt, while talking with our missionary, that God would have him work in that field. Up to this time he had not been taught the experience of entire sanctification, as a second work of grace, but after having it explained he saw that all Christians should attain to this experience and began to ask God to give him a clean heart and the Spirit's witness to it. He received the experience August 3, 1908. In speaking of this he says: "The experience made me shout for joy all day long and I had to dance around my room for joy because I knew that all my sin was washed away forever. From that time I have preached to my fellow Christian comrades to seek for the second blessing, and I shall always do so, for I know it is for all to attain in this life, because I have it myself and the Scriptures teach it." As soon as opportunity was given he began to work in our mission, as he felt that our people were his people. On October 20, 1909, he was accepted as a missionary on trial by our Board. He has labored faithfully and made encouraging progress in the study of the language.

Abraham A. Lind

Abraham A. Lind was born in London, England, April 11, 1880. By birth and training he was a Jew He was graduated from a Hebrew institution in Jewish theology and Old Testament languages. When but a boy he went to a magic lantern show in a Jewish mission. The pictures shown were from the Bible, and the last one was a view of the Lord Jesus on the cross. In spite of his prejudice, from that night his opinion concerning Christ was somewhat changed, and he continued to be in an unsettled state of religious views until his conversion.

Brother Lind enlisted in the British army and was sent to India in October, 1903. While engaged as a soldier at Poona he became deeply convicted of sin. While walking down the street he was attracted by the singing of a hymn in the Methodist church and went in. He listened to the sermon and became very angry, thinking that the whole address was delivered for his special benefit. So personal was the sermon that he expected every minute to hear his name called by the preacher. That night he could not sleep. His past life seemed to have been wasted and the future looked hopeless. In this condition of despair he decided that he would kneel and ask the God of his fathers to have mercy on him, and would tell Him that he believed on Jesus Christ, that He is the Messiah, the Savior of the world, and ask for the forgiveness of his sins. After several hours of prayer and struggle with the enemy, at five o'clock in the morning a peace which he had never experienced before took possession of his soul and he knew that he had entered from death into life. This was on his twenty-fourth birthday, April 11, 1904. After his conversion he joined the Methodist Episcopal church and was licensed as a local preacher, December 26, 1907. About four months after his conversion he began to seek the experience of entire sanctification and obtained it in June, 1905. Describing his experience immediately preceding the reception of this blessing he says: "There was an awful emptiness in my soul, and after a while I could not even pray. I thought that I had lost my salvation altogether and was, in a way, sorry that I had come to the altar. I became almost desperate. But suddenly I received such a baptism with the Holy Ghost, such as infilling with divine light and love and joy, that I completely lost control of myself. I jumped over the altar railings and began to run about in the church, jumping over seats and shouting and praising God. Some of the people were shocked and left the church. They said that I had worked myself up into a state of excitement. But it was a strange kind of excitement, seeing it has lasted for several years without abating in the least. Glory be to God! By His grace it never will abate."

On completing his period of service in the army Brother Lind decided to remain in India and engage in mission work. He became acquainted with our missionaries there and expressed a desire to become one of them. He was received into the Free Methodist church in India, March 13, 1910. He is unusually gifted in acquiring languages, having studied English, German, Latin, Greek, five Semetic and seven India languages. He has taught in the Methodist Episcopal mission high school in India. His principal work, since his conversion, has been evangelistic and pastoral, both among the natives and English. Brother Lind was accepted by the Board as one of our missionaries, October 19, 1910.

John and Sadie Jeffries Klein

Rev. and Mrs. John Klein were accepted as missionaries on trial by the Board, in October, 1907, and appointed to go out to India in the fall of 1908. Brother Klein was born in Germany and is a brother of Matthias Klein who is laboring in our mission in Japan. He was converted at the age of twelve years, and received a grammar school education. He joined the Pentecost Bands and labored with them in America until 1901, when he went out to India under them and spent five years as a missionary in that country.

Sadie Jeffries was educated in the public schools in Pennsylvania and spent two terms at a State Normal school. She was converted at the age of sixteen and a few weeks later engaged in evangelistic work with the Pentecost Bands, laboring among them for six years in this country. In 1899 she went out as a missionary to Central India under these Bands. She spent the most of seven years on the field, her work being principally with the famine orphans. While in India she was married to Brother John Klein, and they labored together in the work there for some time.

Because of the condition of their health they returned to America in 1906. They then withdrew from the Bands and joined the Free Methodist church. They made application to our Board in March, 1907, to be accepted as missionaries and sent back to India. At the annual meeting in October, 1907, the Board accepted them on trial for India to be sent out in 1908. About this time they commenced to labor as evangelists in the Free Methodist church and later took work in the Illinois conference as pastors, in which work they are still engaged. For various reasons, principally because of a lack of funds, their going out has been delayed.

Statistics—India

Missionaries regularly appointed by the Board and sent out......23
Missionaries appointed but not sent out........................ 1
Missionaries accepted by the Board while on the field........... 8

    Total...32

CEYLON

Kittie Wood Kumarakulasinghe

Kittie Wood Kumarakulasinghe was born in Lockport, New York, June 14, 1862. Her father was Rev. Levi Wood, of the Genesee conference, who was well known throughout the church. Her mother died when she was only a child, but she was blessed with a good step-mother. From the time she was six years of age until eighteen, she lived at North Chili, New York. In June, 1875, she was converted in Chili Seminary, and at the age of seventeen was graduated from that institution. In the year 1882 she took up work in the office of the *Free Methodist*, remaining there one and a half years. From there she took up evangelistic work. In the summer of 1884 she was entirely sanctified while attending the St. Charles (Illinois) camp-meeting. In 1886 she went to England and there joined the Salvation Army for the purpose of going to India as a missionary, as she had felt a definite call to that work two years before. At the end of five months, in August, 1886; she sailed for India. After having worked in Ceylon for three years she became acquainted with Mr. Kanakanayakam Charles Barr Kumarakulasinghe, who was Tamil Translator to the Governor of Ceylon and an earnest Christian gentleman. After five years they were married. In 1903 Mr. Kumarakulasinghe died, leaving her with three small children. In 1904, thinking it would be best for her children to bring them to America for a time at least, she started. When only a few days out from New York City the children contracted scarlet fever and two of them died at sea and the other in a hospital in New York. Sister Kumarakulasinghe spent a year in America and then returned to the work in Ceylon.

Some time after her marriage she discontinued her work with the Salvation Army. As opportunity afforded and she was able, she continued work among the Ceylonese. For several years she has been very desirous that our Board should take up work in Ceylon and have a school there and a Rest Home for the India missionaries, but the Board has not felt able to assume this financial responsibility. She also de-

sired to be associated with the Board as one of its missionaries, and in October, 1906, she was received as an associate
missionary and given an allowance of $100 a year and an ap-
propriation to meet her traveling expenses. In the fall of 1908
she was discontinued as an associate missionary under our
Board because our church felt that it could not enlarge the
work at that place. She is now working in a school at
Newara, Eliya, Ceylon, and is still hopeful that our Board
will be able to take up work in that needy field. She writes
interesting articles for publication concerning the work in
which she has labored so long and faithfully.

JAPAN

Our work on this field was commenced by Masazi Kaki-hara (Paul), who had been attending Greenville College, Greenville, Illinois, for two years. He was accepted by the Board in October, 1895, and went back to Japan soon after receiving his appointment. The name Paul was given him by the wife of one of our preachers, with whom he became acquainted soon after coming to America, and in whose family he had a home for a short time. The reason for giving him this name was that on his first voyage from Japan to America he was shipwrecked, and while in the sea received the baptism of fire. She associated him with the Apostle Paul, who was shipwrecked, and so gave him the name of Paul, by which he was generally known among our people. After returning to Japan he took up work among his people on the Island of Awaji and while there interested Rev. Teikich Kawabe and Rev. Sasoa in the work, and they were received into the Free Methodist church. Mr. Kakihara continued his labors until the latter part of 1898, when he came back to America and was here during the general conference of that year. He returned to Japan soon after its close, and a little later married a Japanese woman. He did not continue long in mis sionary work under the Board, but left it and engaged in business at Osaka with two other Japanese. They lost money and failed. In the latter part of 1899 or early in 1900 he returned to America to earn money to pay his debts. When last heard from he and his wife were at 17 Concord street, Brooklyn, New York, at a "Japanese Mission Home."

Rev. Teikich Kawabe and wife were accepted as missionaries on trial at a meeting of the Directors of the Missionary Board held October 23, 1906. He was highly recommended by Brother Kakihara, and his labors were much appreciated by the Board. He was afterward recognized as being in full relation to the mission and the Board. When Brother Kakihara left Japan, Brother Kawabe acted in his place and was in charge of the work until the outgoing of Rev. W. F. Mat-thewson. Brother Kakihara having left our work and disappointed our Board and people in America, and our Board not being personally acquainted with Brother Kawabe, at its meeting held October 12, 1899, it took action and advised Brother Kawabe and his associates in the work in Japan to labor with the Christian and Missionary Alliance people. By request of the Board the Secretary sent this advice to Brother Kawabe. No appropriation was made for the work and workers in Japan at this annual meeting. Later a very interesting letter was received from Brother Kawabe, in which he, speaking of himself and coworkers, requested that our Board continue its appropriation for the work and workers in Japan.

In the fall of 1899 the Missionary Secretary, B. Winget, by request of the Board, visited our mission work in India, going on from there to Japan, where he spent several weeks. While there he formed the acquaintance of Brother Kawabe, who was his guide and interpreter, and talked with him regarding conditions which would be expected of him and the workers if the Board should send out missionaries and renew appropriations for the work and workers there. The Secretary was highly pleased with the Christian spirit of Brother Kawabe and his acquiescence to conditions suggested. Upon his return to America, the Secretary gave an account of the conditions of our work in Japan to the Board, and this body took action approving of sending out missionaries. Brother Kawabe has been faithful and loyal to our work and has continued with us until the present time. A further acquaintance with him on the part of our missionaries who are sent out, and also by the Board through correspondence, has given a better knowledge of his work, and has made him more highly appreciated by our people at home and our missionaries in Japan.

Rev. Wesley F. and Mrs. Minnie Matthewson

Rev. and Mrs. W. F. Matthewson were accepted by the General Missionary Board, October 15, 1902, and appointed to go out to Japan. Brother Matthewson was born September 12, 1868, near Franklinville, New York, and is of Scotch descent. His father was a minister in the Genesee conference of the Free Methodist church and received an appointment from the "Laymen's Convention," which sent out the first preachers.

Brother Matthewson was converted at Spring Arbor, Michigan, during a meeting held by his father in 1882. Through the personal influence of Professor David S. Warner, Brother Matthewson was helped to decide for God. He lost his first love, but in a meeting held by Superintendent B. R. Jones and Rev. J. Ellison was reclaimed, and soon after was called to preach the gospel. He was educated at Spring Arbor Seminary, but on account of sickness did not quite complete the last year's course of study. He united with the Ohio conference in 1894 and labored as pastor on the following charges: Edgerton, North Baltimore, Youngstown, one year each, and Rocky River and Cortland, two years each. He had labored one year on the Holland circuit and had just entered upon his second year's pastorate when he was accepted as a missionary. Brother Matthewson has acted as treasurer of his conference, and secretary of the Board of Examiners in the course of study. He was elected delegate to the general conference, which met just before he went to Japan.

Mrs. Matthewson was born near Coldwater, Michigan, December 26, 1867. She was the eldest daughter of Mr. and Mrs. C. S. Wright, of Algansee, Michigan. Her mother was a member of the Free Methodist church. She received a high school education at Coldwater, and spent about nine years as teacher in the schools of Branch county, at first in district schools and later as principal of the Fourth Ward school in Coldwater. Converted in the Methodist Episcopal church shortly before she was fifteen years of age, she remained a member until she was twenty-two, when she united with the Free Methodist church. She was sanctified wholly in June, 1893. She was active in Sunday-school and missionary work and superintended the home Sunday-school for five years previous to her marriage. She was secretary of the W. C. T. U. at Holland, Ohio, and president of the Olive Branch Mission Band there when appointed, with her husband, to labor in Japan.

They were married August 22, 1894. They have three children, the youngest of which was born in Japan. Writing about leaving for that field she said: "I esteem it a great privilege to be permitted to forsake all and follow Jesus to Japan. My great anxiety is to be true to the trust committed to us and win many souls for God." They left Seattle for Japan, January 26, 1903. His time there was taken up largely in looking after temporal affairs connected with the mission, securing property and buildings for the work. Sister Matthewson assisted in the spiritual work as her strength and family cares permitted. He acted as superintendent of the mission while on the field and showed remarkable ability in taking charge of the work, retaining the respect and confidence of his coworkers, both Japanese and missionaries from the home land, and having the unity of the Spirit among them all. His burdens were heavy and his strength failed so that it became necessary for them to return home the latter part of 1908, where they have remained. He is now in better health, but is not considered strong enough at present to return to Japan. He is acting as pastor within the bounds of the Columbia River conference, in the state of Washington.

August Hawkins and Anna C. Millican Youngren

August Hawkins Youngren was born in the southern part of Sweden, November 16, 1869. He was trained by religious parents and the seed sown in his heart in early life left an ineffaceable impression which brought forth good fruit. He came to this country in 1892 and resided a short time in Denver, Colorado. He was converted November 15 or 16, 1893, in a cottage prayer meeting in Skagit City, Washington, and joined the Swedish Methodist Episcopal church. About eighteen months later he earnestly sought and obtained the experience of entire sanctification. He met with much persecution after receiving this experience, and becoming acquainted with the Free Methodists, he felt they were his people and joined them. He attended a Free Methodist camp-meeting held at Skagit, where he met Rev. Alexander Beers. Brother Beers saw that he was a young man of promise and urged him to attend school at Seattle and prepare for his life's work. Accordingly, he entered Seattle Seminary in the fall of 1895, where he faithfully pursued his studies for six years. He had nearly completed his classical course when called to go at once to Japan, having previously applied to the Board to go as a missionary to that country. He had also taken two years in theology and four years in mission studies, in addition to his regular course. In consideration of the extra work done the trustees unanimously gave him a regular diploma from the seminary. During his stay in school he had regular appointments in the city, where he preached in his native tongue, and for two months previous to leaving America, had charge of a Swedish mission in Seattle, where he held services in both English and Swedish.

Anna C. Millican Youngren is the eldest child of William and Alice Millican. She was born at Salem, Oregon, October 19, 1874, where she lived for seven years. Her parents then moved to Goldendale, Washington, where she resided until she was nineteen years old. She was converted when eleven years of age and joined the Methodist Episcopal church. In the fall of 1890 she and her parents united with the Free Methodist church at Goldendale. In 1893 her parents moved to Seattle, in order that their ten children might have a Christian education. The next year she entered Seattle Seminary. She was graduated from the Latin Scientific Course in 1901. She also received thorough instruction on the organ and piano, and taught music for three years. When but fifteen years of age she was called to God's harvest field. Being seriously ill of pneumonia and given up to die by physicians, she covenanted with the Lord to devote her whole life to His work if she was spared. Contrary to expectations she recovered. Later, while attending a students' meeting led by Mrs. Emma Shay, she received a definite call to go as a missionary to Japan. From that hour she held herself consecrated to that work. When the call came from the Missionary Board, by whom she and Mr. Youngren were accepted January 28, 1903, she was willing to go alone to Japan and postpone her marriage to Mr. Youngren, who would join her some time later, although plans were made and the wedding day set. Afterward, it was thought best by the Board to send Mr. Youngren also, so they were married before going. They embarked from Seattle, with Brother and Sister Matthewson, January 26, 1903. Brother and Sister Youngren have labored very acceptably on that field. Sister Youngren's health, some of the time, has been quite poor, but her counsel

and help have been much appreciated. Brother Youngren
has had excellent success in acquiring the language, and after
Brother Matthewson's return to America in 1908, he was appointed by the Board as superintendent of the mission, and
still holds that relation. They especially needed to return on
account of Sister Youngren's health, and the Board granted
them a furlough. They are now on their way and expect to
arrive about June 1. Sister Youngren is a sister of Mrs. C.
Floyd Appleton and Frank R. Millican who have been several
years in China.

Sherman Ellsworth and Rose Loomis Cooper

S. E. Cooper was born in Lukin township, Lawrence county, Illinois, May 20, 1875. His father, David S. Cooper, was
one of the early settlers in that part of the country.

On September 20, 1892, Brother Cooper registered as a student at Greenville College. He was converted a few weeks
later while eating supper in the college dining hall, and at
once entered actively into the religious life of the school. His
conviction for a clean heart was intensified while milking one
of the college cows, which entered a protest against the pro-
ceedings by kicking and upsetting the pail of milk all over his
new clothes. He fell on his knees and prayed for victory
over his evil temper. He at once began to seek the experience
of entire sanctification, and did not cease until he received
the full assurance that the work was done.

In 1896 he was graduated from the four years' business
course, leading to the degree of Bachelor of Commercial
Science. He remained in the college as a student, or assistant teacher in the business department, until June, 1902, acting as private secretary to President Wilson T. Hogue for
several years and also college bookkeeper and office clerk.
In the Free Methodist church in Greenville, April 30, 1899,
he received his call to the gospel ministry and felt that his
life work must be given to strengthen others, according to
Isaiah 61:1-3. Later, he became interested in the Philippines. He took a government examination for appointment,
but was providentially hindered from going out. He accepted
a position as preceptor and assistant principal of Wessington

Springs Seminary under Professor Clark W. Shay, in 1902. Later Professor Shay resigned and he was called to the principalship for the remainder of the school year. At the close of the year he was reelected principal.

Rose Loomis Cooper was born in Fountain, Colorado, January 5, 1878, and spent the winter of 1885-86 in attending the newly opened seminary at Orleans, Nebraska. During that time she was converted and joined the Free Methodist church. She was sanctified wholly in the fall of 1887 during the session of the Colorado annual conference. She continued her studies in the Fountain public schools from 1886 to 1893, when she entered the high school at Colorado Springs. After two years there she went to Greenville College, where she was graduated from the classical preparatory department in 1897. She then took two years of the college course. In the fall of 1899 she began teaching in Seattle Seminary and continued for three years. The most of the time while there she had charge of the girls in their hall. Following this she taught two years in Wessington Springs Seminary and acted as preceptress for a year and a half.

They were married June 30, 1903, and in September following he joined the South Dakota conference on trial. Brother Cooper having accepted the principalship of the business department of Greenville College, they went there in the spring of 1904 and the same year he was given a circuit in the Central Illinois conference. In addition to the duties connected with these responsibilities, he became business manager of the new college paper, *The Vista*, which was launched during that school year. He also carried some work in the college curriculum. Sister Cooper took up college work where she had left off five years previous and completed one more year in the classical course.

Having been disappointed in going out to the Philippines, they gave themselves to much prayer and careful deliberation, after which they offered themselves to the Board for work in Japan. They were accepted at the annual meeting in October, 1905, and sailed from Seattle, February 1, 1906, arriving at Kobe, February 23.

Upon reaching Japan they entered heartily into the work, especially in studying the language, and success has crowned

their efforts. Two daughters have been born to them since
they went to Japan. Brother Cooper has acted as treasurer
of the mission since Brother Matthewson returned home, and
has been very thorough in his work. They are now in charge
of a station at Akashi where Sister Cooper is doing very successful work among the women and children.

Miss Minnie K. Hessler

Miss Hessler was born in Onondaga county, New York,
February 18, 1884. She was brought up on a farm and attended district school until fifteen years of age. At eighteen
she was graduated from the East Syracuse high school and
spent the following four years teaching in the rural schools
in her home county. She sought the Lord when about nine
years of age, but did not get a satisfactory Christian experience until eleven years later. Soon afterward she was sanctified wholly. From early childhood she felt a desire to be a
missionary, and as the years passed this desire increased un
til she felt assured that this was to be her work. She was
accepted by the Board and appointed to Japan, embark-
ing for that field October 26, 1907, where she has since labored with success. She has taught the young women in the
training school at Osaka and has done evangelistic work, in
which field she is now engaged. For some years she was the
only unmarried person in our mission in Japan. Three of her
brothers are preachers in the Susquehanna conference of the
Free Methodist church.

William Lambie and Grace Livingston Meikle

Rev. William L. Meikle and wife were accepted and appointed by the Board to Japan at its meeting held in October,
1908, and the 29th of the month left for that field.

Brother Meikle was born in Caledonia, Wisconsin, March
14, 1870. His parents were born in Scotland and were members of the United Presbyterian church. Brother Meikle is
the oldest of seven children and was converted to God in answer to the prayers of his mother in their own home in the
summer of 1889. He did not retain a clear Christian experi-

ence, but later, under the labors of Miss C. S. Jenkins, now Mrs. L. B. Webb, his experience was renewed. He soon united with the Free Methodist church and received a license to exhort; later he received a local preacher's license. He joined the Wisconsin conference and served as pastor on the following circuits: Montfort and Fennimore, Platteville, Albany, Evansville, Milwaukee (Second Church), Portage and Caledonia, besides engaging in various lines of Christian work in Wisconsin and Oklahoma Territory. He taught school in the home land.

Grace Livingston Meikle was born in Livingston, Wisconsin, February 3, 1872. She is the youngest of ten children. Her mother is above eighty years of age and is a member of the Free Methodist church. Sister Meikle was converted during a revival held in Livingston by F. F. Wolfe, and soon after united with the Free Methodist church. She was educated in the public schools, in the State Normal at Platteville, Wisconsin, and spent a short time in our seminary at Evansville. She taught school for some time. She was married to William L. Meikle, January 28, 1897. They have four sons, the oldest being eleven years of age, and the youngest about five.

Since their arrival in Japan Brother Meikle has successfully grappled with the Japanese language and is making encouraging progress. He has taught in a training school and done evangelistic work, with good results. Sister Meikle has had many home cares and her health has not been very good, so she has been unable to do much regular missionary work. Most, or all, of the time since their arrival in Japan they have been laboring in the city of Osaka.

Rev. Matthias and Mrs. Harriet C. Klein

Brother Klein was born in Alsace, Loraine (Germany), where he was converted among the Evangelicals at the age of fifteen. He came to America when sixteen years old. He joined the First Free Methodist church, located on May street, Chicago, Illinois, soon after, but lost his Christian experience, and his connection with the church was severed. While living in Indiana he was reclaimed, and coming in touch with the Pentecost Band people, became one of their workers. This was when he was twenty years of age, and he continued his relation with them for about twelve years. He was graduated from the common schools in Germany and his further education has been by private study at home.

Sister Klein was born in Wisconsin and was graduated from high school in Lovington, Illinois. She was converted in a meeting held by Revs. S. B. Ulyness and E. G. Cryer in 1889. She soon became a worker in the Pentecost Bands, where she continued for sixteen years. Some time after joining the Pentecost bands they were married. Not feeling satisfied with their relations, they left the Pentecost Bands and went to Japan as missionaries, expecting to be associated with a certain holiness movement in America which had sent out missionaries to Tokyo, Japan. After arriving in Japan they were disappointed in regard to an expected opening for them there and went to Choshi, Shimosa, Japan, where they labored as independent faith missionaries for a year or more. They then offered themselves to our Board and were accepted on trial in the spring of 1908 and later were admitted as full members of the mission. They have been laboring zealously and acceptably with our workers since that time. Sister Klein has many family cares, which prevent her from doing much regular missionary work. They are now laboring at Sumoto on the Island of Awaji. Since his acceptance by our Board, Brother Klein has united with the Illinois conference in the home land and is recognized as an ordained preacher in the church. Brother and Sister Klein have a family of four children.

Miss Ruth Mylander

Miss Mylander was born on her father's farm near North Platte, Nebraska, August 2, 1881. In the fall of 1889 she entered the North Platte high school from which she was graduated in the spring of 1903. In the fall of that year she entered the Nebraska Wesleyan University where she was graduated in 1907. She went to Greenville College in the fall of 1908 and spent a year studying the Bible and related subjects. At nine years of age she accepted Jesus as her personal Savior, but did not retain a clear Christian experience.

Being afterward reclaimed, she pressed forward, and in the fall of 1907 obtained the experience of entire sanctification. She joined the Free Methodist church in the summer of 1909. Her drawings toward the missionary field commenced in her youth, and while attending the Wesleyan University she became a member of the Student Volunteer Band. Having been accepted by our Board, and appointed to go out to Japan, she left for that field, November 17, 1909. Her father has a very commendable and practical interest in foreign missions which is shown by providing means to send his daughter to Japan and supporting her on the field. With enough such fathers in the church, doubtless the gospel might be given to the whole world in this generation.

Since arriving in Japan, Miss Mylander has given diligence to the study of the language. She is associated with Miss Hessler in the work connected with the young ladies' training school in Osaka and is doing well.

Statistics—Japan

Missionaries regularly appointed and sent out.....................11
Missionaries accepted on the field...............................2
Total..13

CHINA

Miss Clara Leffingwell

Clara Leffingwell was born at Napoli, Cattaraugus county, New York, December 2, 1862. She was the tenth child of Edwin Leffingwell, M. D., and Lorando Merchant Leffingwell. She was an unusual child, thoughtful, religious, and wise beyond her years, giving her life to the service of the Master in her youth. She received the experience of full salvation under the labors of Rev. John Harmon in 1884. For some years she was in poor health and her mind at times was much exercised in prayer for the healing of her body. In the early spring of 1885 she was enabled to take the Lord as her healer and felt a special call to labor for Him in a public way.

In the latter part of 1886 she received her first license to preach by the Chautauqua district, Genesee conference of the Free Methodist church. For some years she taught school in the country where she was permitted to use the schoolhouse evenings and Sundays for religious services, as well as for special revival meetings; so her first ministerial labors were associated with her work as teacher.

She attended the Chamberlain Institute at Randolph, New York, which for many years had been the leading educational center for western New York. In 1887-'88 she attended the A. M. Chesbrough Seminary of North Chili, New York. From there she went to St. Louis and entered the Vanguard Training School, but soon returned to western New York where she again began the work of teaching and preaching. During a part of 1889-'90 she taught at Great Valley and as a result of her labors there as a minister a Free Methodist class was organized. During 1891 she went to Illinois and worked about six months with the Pentecost Bands. For two years following she was engaged in teaching school and preaching in the vicinity of Eldred, Pennsylvania, where she laid the foundation for a large and flourishing work of the Lord. During a part of 1894 she engaged in mission work in the city of Erie, Pennsylvania. In the fall of that year she was appointed pastor at Davis, West Virginia, by the Pittsburg conference of the Free Methodist church.

For some years previous to this Miss Leffingwell's mind had been exercised in regard to going to the foreign field, and in 1895 she was clearly persuaded that God would have her offer her services for mission work in China. About that time she wrote to the Secretary of our Missionary Board in regard to going out under its auspices as a missionary to China. Being informed that the way did not seem open for the Board to send her to China to establish a mission at that time, because of its accepted responsibilities for other fields, she applied to the China Inland Mission. Early in the fall of 1895 she went to the Training Home of the China Inland Mission at Toronto, Canada, and was accepted by that organization November 20, and appointed to go out to China. She, with others, left Toronto, for the Pacific Coast, December 23 and sailed from Tacoma January 5, 1896, arriving at Shanghai, January 30. The party remained a short time at Shanghai and from there went to the Training School of the China Inland Mission, where they spent some time in preparation for their work. Later Sister Leffingwell was sent into the interior, which was her field of labor during most of the time while in China. She passed through some very thrilling experiences in connection with the Boxer trouble and massacres and was wonderfully preserved. At the end of seven years, April 12, 1903, she embarked at Shanghai for the home land, arriving at Seattle in May.

In October, 1899, the Missionary Board of the Free Methodist church instructed its secretary to correspond with Miss Leffingwell in regard to the advisability and cost of establishing a mission station in China and report at the annual meeting in 1900. About that time the attention of some prominent ministers and others in the church was turned toward China. The next action of the Board, according to the record, was June 17, 1903, when it ordered the Secretary to establish a mission in China as soon as convenient, by sending out three missionaries. It further voted that Clara Leffingwell be authorized to travel throughout the church, hold meetings, and raise money for this purpose, and turn all money over to the General Treasurer. She was to labor under the direction of the Missionary Secretary. She spent about eighteen months, or two years, in such labors, especially in the Free Methodist church, in public meetings and personally working to raise funds and secure desirable missionaries. The persons accepted by the Board and appointed to go out with Sister Leffingwell were Rev. N. S. and Mrs. Alice Honn, Miss Florence B. Myers, Miss Edith Graves, Miss Lily Peterson and Mr. George H. Scofield. The party did not go out together, as had been expected, and Miss Peterson did not go out until a year or more later.

Sisters Leffingwell, Myers and Graves left Seattle for China, April 7, 1905, which brought them to Shanghai, May 7. On the 15th they started for the interior. The party went up the Yangste River over six hundred miles. They wore native dress and were expected to eat Chinese food, using chop sticks instead of knives and forks. They arrived at Cheng Chow, May 17, 1905, about noon of the second day after leaving Hankow. October 18, 1904, Sister Leffingwell was appointed superintendent of the China Mission and given power of attorney for that country. Having decided to locate our first mission at Cheng Chow, a compound was rented and occupied by the three women near the north gate of the city. The buildings of that compound were said to be about two hundred years old. Sister Leffingwell's two assistants were without experience and unacquainted with the language, so could not render her much assistance in the work at first. They rented the house June 2, when the hot weather was upon them. Sister Leffingwell was very diligent in preparing for their work until July 4, when she was taken violently ill and died on Sunday, the 16th. The news of her death was a great surprise to the Missionary Board and her many friends in the home land, and was a greater blow, doubtless, to her coworkers in China. It was hoped that she would live long to labor among the Chinese people, whom she so dearly loved and for whom she had made so many sacrifices. She rests from her labors, and her works do follow her. Her hopes had been realized in seeing missionaries from the church of her choice in China and the work commenced. Sister Leffingwell was a remarkable woman and has left the church and others a striking example of devotion and self-sacrifice for the Master's service.

C. Floyd and Laura Millican Appleton

C. Floyd Appleton was accepted by the General Mission-ary Board, October 16, 1903, and appointed to go out to China. He left Seattle for that field, December 19, 1904. He was born in Vivian, Ontario, Canada, August 10, 1880. He attended public school until about fifteen years of age and later attended high school at Markham, Ontario. When quite young he began to attend Free Methodist meetings. About that time a total eclipse of the moon one night caused him to be alarmed and led him to pray earnestly, fearing that the coming of the Lord was at hand.

While attending high school he joined the Canada Meth-odist church and was a faithful attendant at all the services, but was not satisfied with his experience. In 1897 he took a course in the Model Training School for teachers and the next year taught a country school. That same year he united with the Free Methodist church and continued his teaching another year. In the summer of 1900 he went to British Columbia, and from there to Seattle, entering Seattle Seminary in the fall of 1901. He worked his way through this school for two years and sent money home to help those who had kindly aided him in former days. At Seattle Seminary he had a pleasant and profitable time and very helpful associations. While there he labored some in mission work, in the slums of Seattle, and also in the Chinese mission, as God had called him to go as a missionary to China. He returned to his home in Bracebridge in the fall of 1903 and spent a few weeks in the Toronto Bible school, after which he returned to the Pacific Coast. He engaged in work at the carpenter's trade and in doing mission and church work wherever opportunities occurred. In the summer of 1904, as there was a prospect of the first China band being delayed in going out, he entered Greenville College. He was permitted to remain there but a few weeks, when he and Brother Scofield were appointed to China.

Miss Laura Millican was born in Salem, Oregon, and later, with her parents, moved to the state of Washington. She was converted in a Methodist Episcopal revival at Goldendale, Washington, and afterward joined the church. The next sum-mer, at camp-meeting, she sought entire sanctification and

maintained a steady experience for some time. Until about
fifteen years of age she attended the public school and later
assisted her father in his store. Having a good opportunity
to continue in the store, she refused it, as she felt that God
had something better for her, for which she should make
preparation. About this time she and her parents became
identified with the Free Methodist people. Soon after she
passed the necessary examination and received a certificate
for teaching. She began this work at the age of seventeen
in a country school. Having saved some money, and knowing of Seattle Seminary, she planned to attend this school.
She was very desirous of having the entire family go to Seattle in order that the children, ten in number, might have better school privileges. In the fall she entered the seminary
as a student and taught some in the intermediate department for two years. During that time she was definitely
called to public work for the Master and diligently followed
her convictions by engaging in special religious work in Sunday-schools, children's meetings and at camp-meetings. In
1898 she was graduated from Seattle Seminary and went to
Greenville College, Illinois, where she was graduated in 1902.
She returned to Seattle and taught in the seminary, having
partial oversight of the ladies' hall. During that time she was
granted an evangelist's license by the annual conference, and
the following summer assisted in a series of meetings near
Seattle. She also taught English in a Chinese night school
for a time during that season, a work in which she had previously been engaged. She spent a year in the University of
Washington and in the summer school following took work
in English. The next year she was instructor in English and
German in the seminary and had full charge of the ladies'
hall. She sustained this relation for two years and during
that time assisted some in the Seattle City Mission.

After this thorough preparation for her life work, in October, 1905, the Board received her as its missionary and
appointed her to China. She left Seattle, February 1, 1906.
Upon her arrival in China she commenced the study of the
language and acquired the same rapidly, so that within a year
and three or four months she passed the second year's examination and had made a good beginning in the third year.

About this time a request was made to the Board at its meeting in June, 1907, that Brother Appleton and she be permitted to marry. Our rule on marriage requires persons, who go out single, to delay marriage for two years and make good progress in the study of the language, unless by special action of the Board they are permitted to marry sooner; therefore, this special request was granted by the Board. This was about a year and a half after their arrival in China. Previous to their marriage, Brother Appleton had traveled considerable in China in order to gain useful information for assisting him and his coworkers in the difficult task of locating and establishing a mission. The Board appointed Brother Appleton to take the place of Sister Leffingwell as superintendent, in which position he was continued until his return home in May, 1910. Brother Appleton was active and diligent in different lines of work connected with his relation to the mission and had success in acquiring the language. Sister Appleton acted as treasurer of the mission for some time previous to their return to America. The station where they were located at the time of leaving China was Kai Feng Fu, Province of Honan. A severe attack of typhoid fever, from which Brother Appleton did not recover fully, was the immediate cause of their return to America. His health has improved since their return, and they have labored acceptably in the interest of our work in China. They are now making their home at Seattle, Washington. It is hoped that they may be able to return soon.

George Henry and Florence R. Myers Scofield

Brother and Sister Scofield were accepted by the Board, September 5, 1904, and appointed to go out to China as soon as possible.

George Henry Scofield was born in Stanford, Connecticut, in August, 1879. He attended the public school in that place, also spent one year in high school. In his early teens he felt a special call to God's work, but did not obey. He worked four years as an apprentice in a New York trade school and received a diploma with high grades. While attending the trade school, January 24, 1897, he gave his heart and life to

God, and at that time felt the renewed call of the Lord. On December 13, 1899, he received the baptism of the Holy Ghost and fire. January, 1902, he went to Taylor University, Upland, Indiana, and entered upon a theological course. The latter part of March, in the same year, the Lord spoke to him about going to China as a missionary and his heart responded. Since then his love for the Chinese has deepened into a real passion for the souls of these darkened people. He joined the Student Volunteer Band in Taylor University. From the time of his conversion he was diligent in doing personal work in missions and slums, taught in the Sunday-school, held street meetings, etc.

Brother Scofield left Seattle for China, December 19, 1904, in company with Brother Appleton and a missionary of the China Inland Mission, with whom they had become acquainted before leaving America. This missionary gave them special help after they arrived on their field of labor. The mission not being located nor established, Brother Scofield spent some time with Brother Appleton in traveling about to find a desirable place for locating the mission, and also in procuring some helpful knowledge of the people and of mission work among them. When Sister Leffingwell located the mission at Cheng Chow, Province of Honan, these brethren were west of there. After her death they came to Cheng Chow and assisted in making necessary preparation for the establishment of the station and carrying on the work of the mission. Brother Scofield applied himself diligently to the study of the language and met with success, considering his feeble condition of health a part of the time.

Miss Florence Myers was born in Howard, Indiana, in 1879, and was one of a large family of children. Her father was not a Christian in her early life. When nine years of age she received a very definite impression that she was to be a foreign missionary, but was not converted until twenty years of age. Although she had prepared herself for the work of teaching school, God so closed up her way in that direction that she could not proceed in that line of work. A year from the time she was converted, the Lord gloriously sanctified her and made His will very plain. She prepared to attend Taylor University, but did not see definitely how this plan could be carried out, but on the day that she confessed before her father her definite call to the foreign missionary work, he was converted, and the Lord opened her way to attend the university. She spent two years at this school and then taught in the Hadley Industrial School for Girls, where her labors were made a special blessing, a large number of the girls being converted while she was in charge.

Miss Myers went out to China with Miss Leffingwell and Miss Graves, April 7, 1905. After a very trying journey from Shanghai, they reached Cheng Chow in the beginning of the hot season, and she went through some very trying experiences in connection with the beginning of the mission and the sickness and death of Sister Leffingwell. Later, when Brother Scofield and Brother Appleton arrived there, needed assistance was given her and Sister Graves and provision was made for them to commence the study of the language and do some mission work. She was faithful in doing both and had success in acquiring the language. In the following year, 1906, Brother Scofield and Sister Myers were married. Their marriage took place sooner than is usually expected of our missionaries after arriving on the field, but it was thought by those associated with them that there was a special emergency making their case an exception to our rule. After their marriage they took charge of a station and labored very zealously in the work.

The first Free Methodist class in our mission in China was formed on Brother Scofield's station, and they were encouraged by seeing special fruit of their labors. Brother Scofield and his little son had typhoid fever and because of impaired health, and his wife's health being poor, they were granted a furlough and returned home with their two children, leaving China, November 22, 1910. His health is much improved and Sister Scofield is renewed in strength. He has been able to do some acceptable public work in the interest of the work in China. They are looking forward with joyful expectation to returning the latter part of this year.

Rev. N. S. and Alice G. Honn

N. S. Honn and wife were accepted by the Board, October 18, 1904, and appointed to go out to China, but the time of their going out was necessarily delayed until September 6, 1905.

Brother Honn was born in Garden Grove, Iowa, September 4, 1866. In 1886 he first heard of the Free Methodist people, and the following winter, while teaching school, he received the pardoning favor of the Lord. Later, the Spirit led him into the experience of full salvation. Following this came some special persecutions from associates, but they only drove him nearer to the Lord. About this time the Lord spoke to him about going to the heathen Chinese and he was fully persuaded that he was to work among these people. He was received into the church, licensed to preach and appointed to a circuit. He served as pastor for three years in Iowa. In March, 1893, he went to California, where he labored for twelve years previous to going to China. About half of this time he worked among the Chinese on the Coast. He studied their language and largely mastered the gospels and other portions of the New Testament in Chinese. This enabled him to converse with the people and to expound portions of the gospels. When the Missionary Board decided to commence work in China, he sent in an application for himself and wife for appointment to that field.

Sister Honn was born October 5, 1871, at Oneida, Illinois. She is a sister of Rev. G. W. Griffith, who is now principal of our seminary at Wessington Springs, South Dakota. She was clearly converted at fourteen years of age and united with the Methodist Episcopal church. About that time her parents were led to seek the experience of entire holiness, which had its effect upon her, by leading her to take the plain, simple way, although at that time she was attending high school and was the only plainly dressed scholar in the school. In 1887 she became acquainted with the Free Methodists, and immediately felt they were her people. Later, she and her parents united with the church. She and Brother Honn were united in marriage, March 29, 1892. At that time he was a traveling minister in the West Iowa conference. She was heartily with him in his work as an itinerant preacher and also in his labors among the Chinese on the Coast previous to their going to China.

Brother Honn's acquaintance and labors with the Chinese

in America gave him special preparation for work after arriving on the field. They have been diligent in the work and are having their hearts' desire realized in seeking the lost ones on that needy field. When they went to China they had six children, two of whom remained with friends in California in order to attend school. One child has been born since their arrival on the field.

Miss Edith Graves

Miss Graves was accepted by the Missionary Board conditionally, November 17, 1904, and embarked for China, April 7, 1905, going out with Sisters Leffingwell and Florence Myers. She was born November 5, 1876, at Minnesota Lake, Minnesota, and was the eighth of a family of ten children. At the age of twelve her parents moved to Oregon. When seventeen years of age she taught her first school. She was converted August 21, 1893, at the Tremont camp-meeting. After teaching another year, she entered Seattle Seminary, in the fall of 1897. Having to work her way through the seminary, it took a longer time to complete her work. She was sanctified in October, 1900, and received her call to go to China as a missionary the previous year. The love of Christ constrained her to respond to the call of the Master. She taught school for four years after finishing her work in the seminary, and felt that this was a helpful preparation for her work.

After arriving in China with Sisters Leffingwell and Myers, she passed through some very trying experiences while assisting in the establishing of the mission, and in connection with the death of Sister Leffingwell. Her health became impaired and for some time she was unable to pursue her studies successfully. At length, because of illness, it seemed imperatively necessary for her to return home, and she arrived in America in the latter part of 1907 or early in 1908. Her health has improved and she has done some public work to aid the mission in China. Her heart is still enlisted in this cause, and it would give her great joy to be fully restored and able to resume work in China successfuly. Her relation to the Board was discontinued at the annual meeting in 1910, as it was not thought that her health would permit of her again going out.

Miss Lily M. Peterson

Miss Peterson went out to China, February 1, 1906, in company with Laura Millican, and Rev. S. E. Cooper and wife, whose field of labor was Japan. She was first accepted by the Board and appointed to go out with Sisters Leffingwell, Myers and Graves, but because of poor health did not go at that time. The prospect not looking favorable for going out, she sent her resignation to the Board, and it was accepted, October 11, 1905.

Miss Peterson was born in Portland, Oregon. Later her parents moved to Seattle, where they have since lived. She attended Evansville Seminary for two years, 1892-'94, and then returned to Seattle, where she finished her course in Seattle Seminary in 1897. After graduating she remained at home one year and later taught public school for about three years in the state of Washington. The following two and a half years she had charge of one of the departments in the assessor's office at the Kings county court house, Seattle. While attending Evansville Seminary, January 14, 1894, she was converted. At that time she was especially impressed to keep herself free to follow the will of the Lord in all things. Referring to her experience she said it seemed as though she had three calls, or rather three stages to her call, and especially felt that God would have her go as a missionary to China. For some time she taught in the Chinese mission at Seattle, thinking this would be a helpful preparation for her work among that people in their own country. Some of the Chinese were converted. Although she had resigned her relation to the Board, her conviction that God had called her to that field remained, and under the inspiration in connection with the outgoing of Sister Laura Millican and Brother and Sister Cooper, her faith led her to embark with them and go to China. After arriving on the field she sent in her application to the Board and was again accepted, April 12, 1906.

She labored with diligence and success both in acquiring the language and in missionary work after her arrival in China, and was highly appreciated by her coworkers. An inviting field was open to her and she joyfully entered upon her God-given work. One reason of her going at this time was that her friends at Seattle, who had known of her call

and desire to go as a missionary to China, rallied to her support and pledged the necessary funds to pay her allowance
on the field. She was of good courage and her letters home
sounded the notes of victory. It is said she acquired the language with ease and became a general favorite among the
Chinese. They called her their "Pehi-ueh-tean" (white precious lily). After remaining on the field a little over two
years she was taken with fever and was tenderly nursed by
her colaborer, Miss Millican. She appeared to improve and
returned to her station and resumed work. She contended
bravely against the disease, which did not let go its hold
upon her. Finally she was warned by the physicians that her
lungs were seriously affected. With great reluctance she
wrote her loved ones of her condition, bade a sad farewell
to her dear China and turned her face homeward. In the
midst of this sad experience her heart was comforted with the
words of the Master, "Let not your heart be troubled." This
motto, with many other promises, hung at the foot of her
bed during her illness. She reached Seattle, Washington,
March 16, 1908, and was in too feeble a condition to leave
home again. All means and agencies that love could desire or
money purchase were spent for her restoration. The elders
of the church were called and much of God's blessing was
realized in the anointing service. She was relieved, but the
insidious disease continued to make inroads upon her already
over-worn constitution. She failed rapidly, and peacefully
fell asleep in Jesus, June 4, 1908, just a little more than two
years from the time she reached China. The last two nights
of her life she was partly delirious and talked very fluently in
the Chinese tongue. This showed that her heart was in China.
She was eager to depart and be with Christ. When one of
her friends urged her not to look toward the grave, she re-
plied: "Oh, I am looking right up to heaven and I see Jesus
close by." Brother and Sister Peterson, who have given so
generously of their means to establish a work in China, also
gave their first-born child and murmured not when God took
her to Himself. Her sweet influence will never die. She has
left an example which will be an inspiration to others. Doubtless her mantle has fallen upon her Sister, Mattie, who since
her death has gone out to take her place in China.

Lucy A. Tittemore

Miss Tittemore was accepted by the Board and appointed to China, October 12, 1905, but for several reasons, especially lack of funds, her outgoing was delayed until October 26, 1907. She was born at St. Armand Centre, Province of Quebec, Canada, August 10, 1879. She attended the district school and the Frelighsburg Model School. She passed the teachers' examination in 1897 and taught school four years in the Province of Quebec. When sixteen years old she was converted in revival services held in the Methodist church of Canada. At the age of twenty, having become acquainted with the Free Methodist people, she united with them. She entered into the experience of entire sanctification at a Free Methodist camp-meeting held in her father's grove in August, 1897. She was graduated from the Christian Workers' Course of the A. M. Chesbrough Seminary in 1904. She dates her special conviction for work in China from hearing Miss Clara Leffingwell speak at Glens Falls, New York, in September of 1903. So strong were her convictions that God would have her go to China that she felt to go to any other field would be equivalent to staying at home. Since her arrival in China she has enjoyed very good health, has been diligent in studying the language and is encouraged in her work.

Miss Edith Frances Jones

Miss Edith Jones was conditionally accepted and appointed to China, March 19, 1907. She went out, leaving Seattle, October 26, 1907, being accompanied by Miss Tittemore and Mr. and Mrs. Frank R. Millican.

Miss Jones was born in Jamestown, New York. She was converted in early life and for some years has been a member of the Free Methodist church. She was graduated from Syracuse University, in Syracuse, New York. She taught in Greenville College for two years before going to China and was very highly esteemed for her work's sake in the home land. While at Greenville she was a member of the Student Volunteer Band. Upon her arrival in China she applied herself diligently to the study of the language and has made excellent progress. She has also rendered valuable assistance

to some of our missionaries in acting as nurse during serious
illness. When it became necessary for Brother and Sister
Appleton to return home, Sister Jones was appointed treasurer of mission funds in the place of Sister Appleton, which
office she has filled most acceptably.

Frank Richard and Aimee Boddy Millican

The applications of Frank R. Millican and wife were pre
sented to the Board, March 17, 1907, and received favorable
consideration. They were accepted later and left for China,
October 26, 1907. Brother Millican was born near Goldendale, Washington, November 7, 1883, and is a brother of Sisters Appleton and Youngren, and of Roy W. Millican, an accepted candidate for China. He entered Seattle Seminary,
November 7, 1893, at the age of ten years, and was graduated
from that institution in the spring of 1902. Soon after entering the seminary he was converted and sanctified wholly.
He entered Greenville College in the fall of 1903 and spent
two years there. Part of the year preceding his going to
Greenville, and the year following his return from there, he
spent in the University of Washington, Seattle. His work in
the university was interrupted by failure of health the first
year and the last year in order to accept the pastorate of the
Buckley and Lake Tapps circuit, Washington, the pastor of
that circuit, Rev. George Edwards, having left his work to go
as a missionary to India. Brother Millican acknowledges
that, next to the mercy of God and the kindness of parents,
he is indebted to Christian schools and self-sacrificing Christian teachers.

Mrs. Aimee Boddy Millican was born in Burkley, California, in 1884. She was definitely converted at the age of seven,
and at twelve years of age joined the Free Methodist church.
Her father, Rev. William Boddy, was a minister in the
church and was transferred to the Washington conference.
She entered Seattle Seminary, and while there as student
was wholly sanctified, and did some work among the Chinese
of the city. While doing this work, she felt that God would
have her go to China. She was graduated from the seminary
in 1905, and taught there for one year. They were married

some time before being accepted by the Board. Since their arrival in China they have labored faithfully and have made excellent progress in acquiring the language. Since the return home of C. Floyd Appleton Brother Millican has acted as superintendent of the mission.

George Donald and Mary Christine Schlosser

George D. Schlosser went from Africa to China in 1908, by permission and appointment of the Missionary Board, having had previous conviction that China was his God-given field of labor. He was born in Chester county, Missouri, December 15, 1875, and is of Scotch-German descent. His father was a Union soldier during the Civil War. In the spring of 1882 he moved to Dakota. He is one of a family of twelve children, seven boys and five girls. His first schooling began when eight years of age, and was in a mud house with a thatched roof. The school lasted about ten weeks each winter, and he attended until he was twenty-one. At that time Dakota was visited by many hail storms, fires and drouths, which made it hard for his parents and himself. He attended the South Dakota Agricultural College. Later he joined the First South Dakota Infantry of the U. S. Volunteers as Sergeant in Company K, on May 4, 1898. He had many trials in the army, but received special help from the Lord. His soldier life was spent in the Philippines. He returned from there October 5, 1899, and resumed his work on the farm and taught school. In 1903 he went to the state of Washington and while there took a course in horticulture in the State Agricultural College and worked at orcharding, etc.

In early years, at home, Brother Schlosser was taught that he could not know that he was saved, but he found the Lord as his forgiving Savior when all alone and many miles from home. The Lord brought him out later into the experience of full salvation and established his goings. He spent some time as a student at Greenville College, Illinois, and was there at the time he was accepted and appointed as a missionary to Africa. He has labored both in Africa and China with zeal and acceptability. Because of the imperative need of more help at the Orphanage, soon after arriving in China

he went to Tsing Kiang Pu to assist Brother and Sister
Fletcher in that work.

Mary Christine Ogren was accepted by the Board, October 22, 1908, and went out to China with Miss Mattie J. Peterson, November 17, 1909. She was born at Jamestown, New
York, and attended the public schools in that city. In June,
1908, she was graduated from Greenville College. She was a
member of the Student Volunteer Band at Greenville. She
taught in Sunday-school and led young people's meetings.
Her conversion took place at Randolph, New York, while attending a camp-meeting in August, 1900. Later, she experienced the blessing of perfect love. Her convictions were
strong that the Lord would have her go to China, and upon
arriving on that field she entered very zealously into the
work of studying the language, and assisted as opportunity
afforded in missionary work.

January 13, 1911, she was married to George D. Schlosser,
at the mission station at Cheng Chow, Honan. At the time
of their marriage she had passed the first year's course of study
in the language, and because of the imperative need of another lady missionary to assist in the work at the Orphanage,
the Directors made an exception to the rule on marriage.
Brother and Sister Schlosser are earnestly laboring at the
Orphanage with Brother and Sister Fletcher in caring for the
children and in looking after other work connected with the
erection of necessary buildings, etc. Brother Schlosser is especially in charge of the building work and is acting as treasurer of mission funds sent to that station.

Fred J. and Mabel D. Culbertson Fletcher

Fred J. Fletcher and wife did not go out to China under
appointment by our General Missionary Board, they having
gone out at the time of the famine in 1907. Being in the famine section and laboring for the welfare of the famine stricken
people, when Brother Appleton, as superintendent of our mission, went to that field, he formed their acquaintance. Later
he wrote to the Secretary of the Board concerning the proposition made by the Famine Committee of the *Christian Herald*
in regard to different missions accepting the responsibility of

caring for orphans who had been rescued by famine funds sent out by the *Christian Herald*. His proposition included the acceptance by our Board of Brother and Sister Fletcher and giving them charge, under our superintendent, of the Orphanage. The Directors took favorable action and Brother and Sister Fletcher were received and appointed to this work, where they have continued to labor.

Brother Fletcher was born in Massachusetts, but lived for many years in Michigan. His father was a Congregational minister and went out to India as a missionary under the American Board when it took himself and wife five months on a sailing vessel to reach his field of labor from New York. They remained in India only five years because of poor health. When about twenty-three years of age Brother Fletcher left Michigan for the West, stopping first at Portland, Oregon. From there he went to Tacoma, Washington, where he lived for fifteen years or more before going to China. The most of the time while at Tacoma he was a member of the Congregational church, a deacon, superintendent of the Sunday-school and very active in church work. He attended some meetings held by Dr. Carradine and was led into the experience of full salvation and felt that the Lord would have him give his services for the foreign missionary work.

Mabel D. Culbertson was born in Iowa, February 21, 1873. Her parents were members of the Methodist Episcopal church and later of the Holiness Association. She was brought up very religiously and was thoroughly instructed in Methodist doctrines. At the age of fifteen she taught in Sabbath school and two years later was taken into the church. She lost her Christian experience, but was restored to the favor of God, and about four years afterward sought and obtained the experience of entire sanctification. In connection with receiving this experience there came an intensified desire to be useful in the Master's vineyard and she commenced to labor in mission work in Sioux City, Iowa, where she then lived. Later she went to Tacoma, and becoming acquainted with the Free Methodists felt that they were her people. She became one of them and was secretary of the Woman's Foreign Missionary Society of the Tacoma district and president of the Tacoma local society. She was also superintendent of the Sunday-school, being very zealous for the Lord. While there she spent ten months in the Tacoma Gospel Mission work as assistant superintendent, where services were held every evening and Sunday afternoons. Her heart was strongly drawn out in love for the heathen and she felt that God called her to be a missionary to the Chinese.

She was married to Fred J. Fletcher a short time before leaving for China. Since their acceptance by our Board their labors have been at Tsing Kiang Pu, where our orphanage is located. They were the special agents in connection with the beginning of that work, and since that time, probably, have had more responsibility and have given more service in connection with caring for the orphans than any of our missionaries in China. Their hearts are in the work and they are full of zeal for the salvation of the children and for the ingathering of jewels for the Master from among the darkened Chinese.

Miss Mattie Josephine Peterson

Miss Peterson was accepted by the Missionary Board and appointed to China, October 22, 1908, and went out, September 17, 1909. She was born at Seattle, Washington. She was converted, February 1, 1898, and the summer following joined the Free Methodist church.

Miss Peterson attended the public schools at Seattle, Seattle Seminary and Greenville College, and was graduated from the last two named institutions. She taught in Sunday-school and did some work at the Chinese mission in Seattle. It was during her senior year at Greenville College that her heart was especially impressed that she ought to go as a foreign missionary to China. In connection with this call she had an ardent love for the heathen, and especially the Chinese. Referring to this she says: "I do not feel that the Lord has imposed an arduous or disagreeable duty upon me by calling me to labor among the heathen. I esteem it an honor that He has deemed me worthy to be a messenger of light to those who are in darkness. My deepest desire is in the Chinese people." It is quite natural that Sister Peterson should be drawn toward the Chinese, as her father has taken such an interest in our missionary work in China and her sister Lily went to that field, and returning home sick, soon passed to her heavenly reward. Brother and Sister Peterson have manifested a self-sacrificing interest in China, not only in giving of their means, but in giving their two daughters as messengers to carry the good tidings to that people. Since arriving in China Sister Peterson has diligently applied herself to the study of the language and has made encouraging progress. Her health has been good and she has been doing faithful service for the Master.

Roy William Millican

At a meeting of the Missionary Board held October 20, 1910, the following action was taken in regard to accepting and sending out Roy W. Millican to China: "On motion, the Secretary is instructed to correspond with Roy Millican regarding his going out to China, and if he can be secured, and if satisfactory recommendations are given, he be sent out by the Secretary." His recommendations were satisfactory and he was appointed to go out and made preparations accordingly; but because of very unexpected circumstances occurring immediately preceding the time he was to embark, his outgoing was delayed and he is still in the home land awaiting further directions from the Board.

Brother Millican was born at Goldendale, Washington, September 23, 1881. His parents afterward moved to Seattle, Washington, where he attended the city schools and also Seattle Seminary, high school and Greenville College. He has done some special Christian work in teaching in Sunday-school, leading class meeting, young people's meetings and has taught in the Chinese mission night school in Seattle. He was converted in 1894 and soon after joined the Free Methodist church. In 1905 he labored in the legislative campaign for the State Prohibition Committee of Minnesota and in 1908 for the Illinois State Prohibition Committee in the 22d Legislative District. While at Greenville College he spent one year in medical studies under Dr. E. M. Easley, who has charge of the medical missionary training course.

Miss Maud Winifred Edwards

At the time Roy W. Millican and F. D. Helm and wife were accepted conditionally by the Board, further action was taken approving of the Secretary securing other persons to go out to China in case the ones mentioned were not available. As none of these were available, the Secretary wrote to the Directors of the Board sending the application and recommendations of Sister Edwards for their consideration. Having received the approval of the Directors, on April 20, 1911, he informed Sister Edwards that she was accepted and appointed to go out to China. The Secretary thought best to delay her going out until the latter part of August or September. By going then she will reach China at the beginning of the cool season.

Miss Edwards was born at Hume, Allegany county, New York. She attended the common schools and also the A. M. Chesbrough Seminary. She was converted in February, 1896, and joined the Free Methodist church the same year. Later she experienced the blessing of perfect love. Her special Christian work has been teaching in Sunday-school and laboring as an evangelist. Her first conviction for the foreign missionary work dates back to the time when she was a child and heard Sisters Grace Allen and Ida Heffner speak in a missionary meeting. This conviction remained with her and led to her consecration for that work. Home ties prevented her from following her God-given convictions at first, but on December 31, 1907, she consecrated herself fully for missionary work on any field. Referring to her recent experience she says: "To-day I have a burning desire to help spread the gospel in China. I feel confident I am in God's will. This past year has been one of the most joyful years of my life. I would deem it a glorious privilege to spend and be spent, not in an easy place, but in the hard places of the earth for my Master."

Statistics—China

Missionaries regularly appointed and sent out....................16
Missionaries regularly appointed but not sent out................ 2
Missionaries accepted by the Board while on the field 2

Total.. 20

DOMINICAN REPUBLIC

Rev. S.E. Mills

Rev. S. E. Mills and family went out to the Dominican
Republic, West Indies, the latter part of the year 1889. At
that time they were members of the Free Methodist church.
For some time after reaching the field they retained their re
lation to the church, and by request were listed as members
of our General Missionary Board, without salary. Brother
Mills and wife, before uniting with the Free Methodist church,
had been members of the Protestant Episcopal church, but
receiving the experience of entire sanctification, they were led
to change their church relation. They were so filled with zeal
to carry the good tidings to the people in the Dominican Republic that Brother Mills gave up his business and, feeling
the call of the Lord, went to that field. He went out in faith
and has never received his support from our Board or any
other church organization. His support has been principally,
or wholly, provided from means entrusted with him as the
Lord's steward. There have been about two hundred converts as the result of the labors of Brother Mills, Sister Clark
and others on that field. These converts have not been or
ganized into societies and a church. This is largely due to
the fact that Brother Mills does not believe in any denom-
inational organization. He teaches the doctrine of experi-
mental and practical holiness and is a very self-denying, hum-
ble, zealous laborer in the Lord's vineyard. Early in 1898
Brother Mills requested that his name and that of his wife
be dropped from the roster of Free Methodist missionaries,
as they did not feel satisfied to be nominally associated with
any missionary board or church.

Sister Mills departed this life about two years ago, leaving a family of several children. Two of the sons were graduated from our A. M. Chesbrough Seminary. Brother Mills
is still doing missionary work on the island.

Miss Esther D. Clark

Miss Esther D. Clark, of Mentor, Ohio, was educated in
the public schools and in Madison Seminary, after which

she taught school for a few years. When fourteen or fifteen years of age she was converted. Five years later she was sanctified at a holiness camp-meeting and joined the Free Methodist church. From early childhood she had an impression that she would labor as a foreign missionary, but did not hear much on this subject.

Rev. S. E. Mills and wife were acquaintances of hers, and knowing of the work they were doing in the Dominican Republic through correspondence, she became interested in the work and responded to their call for help. By the approval of the Board she left New York for there, August 1, 1893. Her labor has been principally teaching a mission school and doing personal and evangelistic work among the people. The religion of the island is Spanish Roman Catholicism, and the people are not very responsive to the truth, but God has given encouraging fruit from the labors of Brother and Sister Mills, Miss Clark, and some others, who have assisted in the work.

The Board allowed Miss Clark $50 toward her outgoing fare. Because of poor health she left the island and returned home on furlough, arriving in New York, October 12, 1899. She returned in 1904, the Board paying her fare both ways. It again became necessary because of her health to return home, and she arrived in New York, November 24, 1910. From the time she went out in 1904 the Board has granted her small yearly allowances.

Rev. J. W. Winans

Rev. J. W. Winans was accepted by the Missionary Board at its meeting in June, 1907, and it was left with the Missionary Secretary to accept and send him to Santo Domingo if conditions were satisfactory and he thought best. Later, and previous to the annual meeting in October, the Secretary informed him that he was accepted and soon after he left for the Dominican Republic, Santo Domingo. The Board allowed $50 toward his outgoing expenses, but did not accept further financial obligations toward his support and expenses after arriving on the field.

Brother Winans was born May 5, 1864, in Canfield, Ontario, Canada, and received a good common school education. Later he taught school and attended the Northern Indiana normal school for two winters, where he was graduated in shorthand and typewriting. Some years later he attended the Canada business college at Hamilton, Ontario, and was graduated from the same department with honors.

He was converted, December 11, 1898. Three weeks later he received the experience of entire sanctification and since that time has been faithful in the Lord's service. His first conviction regarding going to Central America as a missionary was in August, 1899. Prompted by this call, he sailed for that country July 3, 1891, where he spent three months in Honduras and made several trips into the interior, doing a little missionary work among the English-speaking people and gaining a slight knowledge of the Spanish language. For lack of funds he returned in a short time. In 1902 he was received on trial as a preacher in the West Ontario conference and continued in that work until he left for Santo Domingo, the latter part of 1907. Since arriving there he has diligently studied the language and done considerable evangelistic work. He was well received by the Dominicans and is still laboring there. The Board has granted him small allowances toward living expenses. God is helping him to sow the seed and the promise is it shall not be in vain.

Roy E. and Pauline Silcher Nichols

Roy E. Nichols and wife were accepted by the Board, October 15, 1907, to be sent out to the Dominican Republic when, in the judgment of the Missionary Secretary, funds would permit. They left New York for that field August 7, 1908.

Brother Nichols was born in Isabella county, Michigan, in June, 1878. He was converted and joined the Free Methodist church. In the fall of 1901 he went to the A. M. Chesbrough Seminary and was graduated from the Christian Workers' Course, having previously attended the Clyde (New York) high school. In 1904 he went to Seattle, Washington, and was given an appointment to preach in the Washington conference. The Lord brought him into the experience of entire sanctification in March, 1907.

Pauline Silcher was born in Minnesota and lived there with her parents until seven years of age, when they moved to South Dakota. Her conversion took place February 16, 1894. Soon after this she became especially interested in city mission work and labored some in this work in Minneapolis, Minnesota. Her call to the foreign field was received December 31, 1895. In the spring of 1898 she went to Portland, Oregon, and became acquainted with the Free Methodist people. She felt she was one of them and joined the church. The next five years she attended Seattle Seminary, where she received the blessing of entire sanctification. This experience more fully established her purpose of going to the foreign field whenever opportunity afforded.

She was married to Roy E. Nichols, September 18, 1907. At that time he was supplying a circuit in the Washington conference near Seattle, in order that he might attend the University of Washington for one year. They both felt persuaded that the Lord would have them offer themselves for work in the Dominican Republic, which they did. After arriving on that field they applied themselves to the study of the language, and in connection with this he took a number of evangelistic tours into different parts of the island. They labored faithfully, but his work and responsibilities, in connection with the tropical climate, caused a failure of his health, and with regret they returned home, arriving November 24, 1910. Brother Nichols' health is somewhat improved, but not fully restored. They are now living in Portland, Oregon.

Rev. William C. Willing, M. D.

William C. Willing was accepted by the Board, October 14, 1907, and appointed to go out to the Dominican Republic within a year if the Missionary Secretary thought best. The Board was to pay his expenses to the field, and provide him with medicines and instruments for surgical work. It was expected that after reaching the field enough would be received from his profession as doctor and surgeon to meet his temporal needs.

He was graduated from the Hahneman Medical College, Chicago, and practised medicine for six years. Following this he joined the Illinois conference and took work for eight or nine years immediately preceding his going to the Dominican Republic. He had been deeply interested in missionary work for years previous to his application to the Board, and especially in the Spanish-speaking, Roman Catholic people, and when the call came for workers for the Dominican Republic, he responded. Writing about his call he says: "While practising medicine I was hampered all the time by a call to the work of God. I can have no other calling in life than the ministry of the gospel, but I see no objection to letting these other qualifications help on the work. We are prayerfully in earnest to do something for God and souls."

Some time before going to the Dominican Republic his wife died, but before leaving he was again married and took his wife with him to that field. Upon arrival he commenced the study of the language, which is Spanish, and also began the practise of medicine in connection with missionary work. He did but little missionary work, soon lost his Christian experience and failed to be helpful to the work and coworkers on the field. At a meeting of the Board held October 16, 1909, after hearing a communication from Dr. Willing, and also a reply to the same by the Missionary Secretary, the Board discontinued him as missionary. The last heard they were still on the island, but expected to return home soon.

Miss Nellie Whiffen

An offer of the usual allowance for our missionaries having been made by a friend to support Sister Whiffen as a missionary in the Dominican Republic for an indefinite length of time, and her application and recommendations being satisfactory, she was accepted by the Board and appointed to go out to that field, which she did, in company with Dr. W. C. Willing and wife, June 4, 1908. She was born October 6, 1876, in Fulton, New York. Her father, brother and sister are preachers. The father has been a minister in the Susque-

hanna conference of the Free Methodist church for over forty
years, and her sister is the wife of Rev. F. W. Cathey.

Miss Whiffen had the benefit of high schools in different
places where her father was stationed as pastor, and took
a three years' course in the Oswego State Normal and Training School, from which she was graduated in February, 1898.
Following this she taught one term and then entered the
training school for nurses connected with St. Luke's Hospital
in Utica, New York. She was graduated from that institution in October, 1901. Following her graduation she engaged
in nursing and later cared for her invalid mother for about
three years. After the death of her mother she renewed her
services as a private nurse and also discharged, to some extent, the duties of housekeeper for her father. In December,
1907, she, with Miss Florence Deyle, engaged in evangelistic
work under the direction of District Elder H. W. Fish, of the
Susquehanna conference, and continued in this work up to the
time of leaving for the Dominican Republic.

She was converted at the age of seven years, but did not
retain a clear experience. The joy of salvation was restored
to her at the age of seventeen. Receiving the experience of
full salvation she offered herself for work in the Republic. She has been very successful in acquiring the Spanish language, being able to preach in that tongue in a comparatively short time after arriving on the field. Her labors
among the Dominicans have been much appreciated and fruitful in results. She was associated in labors with Sister Esther
D. Clark. As it became necessary for Sister Clark to return
home, and circumstances seemed unfavorable for Sister Whiffen to remain in the work alone, she considered it an oppor-
tune time for her to return to the States and take a special
course which would prepare her for better work among the
Dominican women. Since her return she has taken a course in
obstetrics and is expecting to return to the island in Septem
ber, accompanied by Miss Florence E. Jolly, of Kansas.

Miss Florence Edna Jolly

According to the action of the Directors of the Missionary
Board at their annual meeting held October 20, 1910, the Mis-

sionary Secretary was authorized to secure and send out a young lady missionary to assist Miss Nellie Whiffen in the Dominican Republic, West Indies. In accordance with this action, he secured Miss Florence E. Jolly for that field. The return home of Miss Whiffen has delayed the time of Sister Jolly's going out, but she is expecting to go with Sister Whiffen the coming September and be associated with her in the work.

Miss Jolly was born in Chase county, Kansas, October 9, 1883. She attended common schools, Orleans Seminary, was graduated from Greenville College preparatory department, and later, in 1910, received the degree of Ph. B. from the same institution. Her conversion took place in the summer of 1891. She did not retain this experience, but was reclaimed in 1900. In the summer of 1894 she united with the Free Methodist church. She was licensed to preach in August, 1902. Since that time she has continued to sustain the relation of evangelist in the Kansas conference. Previous to her attending college she labored as an evangelist and supplied a circuit in Kansas. Soon after her conversion she felt called to foreign work and this conviction increased as the years went by, leading her to offer herself for work in the Dominican Republic. During the past year she has been teaching school.

Statistics—Dominican Republic

Missionaries regularly appointed by the Board and sent out........ 6
Missionaries accepted by the Board, without salary, while on the
    field 2
Missionaries appointed but not sent out.... 1

    Total. . . . .,. 9

NORWAY

Mr. and Mrs. S. V. Ulness and Mr. and Mrs. B. Jensen were accepted as missionaries to Norway by the Board at its annual meeting held October 18, 1892. S. V. Ulness and wife went out to Norway as Pentecost Band missionaries about a year previous to their being accepted by the Board. They came back to America in 1893, and returned after a visit of a few months. Mrs. Ulness withdrew from the Board in 1897, and about a year later he withdrew. They found no fault with the Board, but claimed they had received greater light and blessing, and because of this could not belong to any church nor work under any Board.

INDEX

www.ingramcontent.com/pod-product-compliance
Lightning Source LLC
Chambersburg PA
CBHW021159020426
42331CB00003B/132